the Anglo guide to survival in Québec

the Anglo guide to survival in Québec

Edited by
Josh Freed & Jon Kalina

Eden Press
Montréal · London

SATIRE: a satirical composition. The employment, in speaking or writing, of sarcasm, irony, ridicule, etc., in denouncing, exposing or deriding vice, folly, abuses or evils of any kind. (Shorter Oxford English Dictionary)

THE ANGLO GUIDE TO SURVIVAL IN QUEBEC
Edited by Josh Freed and Jon Kalina

ISBN: 0-920792-33-2

Credits:
Original Cover Illustration: © 1983 Aislin.
Book Design: J.W. Stewart with Evelyne Hertel.
Cartoons courtesy of Aislin, *The Gazette*. Reprinted with permission of The Toronto Star Syndicate.
Photographs in *La Petite Histoire (Version Anglaise)*, courtesy of Nick Auf der Maur.
The following models appeared in the *Adopt an Anglo* photograph:
Francis Salter, Stephen Wetmore, Cathra Horrobin, Jess Dutton and Tsuki the dog. With thanks.
Illustrations for *Montreal Estates, Car Wars* and *Prayer or Profanity* by Bob McGee.
Photographs in *A Voyage East, Adopt an Anglo,* and *Signing Off* by Andrew Blanchard.
Photograph of Les Nirenberg by Howard Cohen

Printed in Canada at Imprimerie Gagné Ltée.
Dépôt légal — quatrième trimestre 1983
Bibliothèque nationale du Québec

Eden Press
4626 St. Catherine Street West
Montreal, Quebec H3Z 1S3

THE CONTRIBUTORS

JOSH FREED works in every medium but the hammer and chisel. He writes for newspapers, magazines, radio and TV, and has authored a book *(Moonwebs)* which became the film *Ticket to Heaven.* He has bankrupted two publishing companies and one newspaper *(The Montreal Star),* and has only one goal remaining in life: never to have to move to Toronto. He is currently working as a regular correspondent for CBC's *The Journal,* but is best known for his extraordinary knowledge of cheap ethnic restaurants in Montreal.

JON KALINA entered the world in 1948, speaking no recognizable language. He soon became an anglophone. Years later, while working as a journalist in Montreal, he became functionally bilingual. He has worked for more than ten years as a journalist, in radio, television and print. He was the host of *Critical Path,* a CBC current affairs TV show, and he hopes that he will be able to continue working after the publication of this book.

AISLIN is the pen-name of Terry Mosher. Originally from Ottawa, Mosher settled in Montreal, where he has been drawing cartoons ever since. Mosher has won a number of awards, including two Canadian Newspaper Awards, 1977 and 1978, the prestigeous Quill Award, and five prizes from the International Salon of Cartoons. Mosher lives in Montreal with his wife, Carol, two daughters, one dog and eight cats.

NICK AUF DER MAUR is a native of Montreal, and currently works as a columnist, broadcaster, and city councillor.

DON ARIOLI immigrated to Canada from Rochester, New York in 1962, and joined the National Film Board as a writer and cartoonist. In 1967 his film *The House That Jack Built* was nominated for an Academy Award, and he received an Etrog at the Canadian Film Awards for writing *Hot Stuff* (1972) and *A Propaganda Message* (1973).

GERRY BERGERON is a New Wave cabinetmaker, producing day-glo, nihilistic furniture for many of Montreal's lowest citizens. He was born in the tiny fishing hamlet of Shawinigan Falls, Quebec.

RON BLUMER is an ex-Montrealer. He is presently making film documentaries for *The Bill Moyer Show* in New York.

MIKE BOONE was born in New Brunswick, and raised in Montreal. He is a professional journalist, rock writer and TV critic at *The Gazette.* He is functionally unilingual, but his wife speaks French and generally answers the phone. He is moving to Pointe Claire, but is not unpacking until the next provincial election.

CHARLES BURY was born and raised in Montreal, and was a founding director of the Council of Quebec Minorities. In 1972 he moved to the Eastern Townships, where he is now the Editor-in-Chief of *The Sherbrooke Record.*

VICTOR DABBY is the product of a trilingual Middle-Eastern family, and is currently trying to teach Arabic to his three-year-old daughter, Dia. He is presently employed as a journalist in Montreal.

GRAEME DECARIE was born and raised in Montreal. He teaches Canadian History at Concordia University. In his spare time he is a free-lance writer, and broadcasts regularly on CBC Radio.

MICHAEL FARBER is a sports columnist at *The Gazette,* where he won the 1982 National Newspaper Award. A 1973 graduate of Rutgers University, Farber lives in Quebec by choice.

SERGE GRENIER was born in Montreal, and, chances are, will die here. He became a humourist while studying philosophy at the Université de Montréal, after discovering that Woody Allen was funnier than Plato. After five long years in Ontario, he returned to Quebec, and is now a full time writer and humourist.

WAYNE GRIGSBY, broadcaster, journalist and critic, has been stepping out in Montreal for more years than he cares to admit. Born in Calgary in 1947, he showed signs of prescience early. In 1950, as the train bringing him to Montreal crossed the Ottawa River, he asked, "What's the name of this country we're going to?"

ROBERT McGEE, a refugee from Gatineau County, has published two collections of verse, and worse, illuminated parts of this manuscript. He lives somewhere in the East End.

KATIE MALLOCH has been knockin' em dead on CBC Radio and television, combining wit, charm and perspicacity with breathtaking modesty. She resides in Montreal and has no plans to jump ship to Hogtown.

KARL NERENBERG is an ex-Montrealer working as a producer for CBC's *The Journal* in Ottawa.

LES NIRENBERG is, at this moment, living the best way he can in Toronto. He is a frequent producer of stories for CBC's *The Journal,* does interviews for the *Subway Review* on CBC Radio's *Variety Tonight,* acts in commercials and runs a thriving industrial video business. He claims it is not an easy thing to be a "Renaissance Man".

KATHRYN O'HARA is a freelance writer, broadcaster and the consumer reporter for CFCF TV's *Pulse News.*

STEPHEN PHIZICKY grew up in Montreal, did terribly in high school French but managed to fake his way through a number of jobs. He is now Montreal producer of CBC's *The Journal,* and still believes that speaking bad French is better than speaking no French at all.

ELAINE SHATENSTEIN was born in Montreal and educated at Sir George Williams and McGill Universities. She is a hired pen by trade and is currently preparing material for a project called "How To Live".

DAVID SHERMAN has led a dull, predictable, Quebec anglophone existence. A journalist by trade, a complainer by habit, he is currently a producer at CBC Radio in Montreal and the father of one Anglo-Franco son.

ELEANOR WACHTEL, born and educated in Montreal, has lived in the US, Kenya, Toronto and, for the last eight years, in Vancouver. She is currently freelancing as a writer, broadcaster, researcher, editor and occasional teacher.

Dedication

On May 1, 1983, Antonio Balducci, a sixty-year-old Montreal man, shot himself at Dorval Airport. A suicide note was found in his pocket explaining that he had been transferred to Scarborough, Ontario. Mr. Balducci did not want to go. *

This book is dedicated to those anglos like Mr. Balducci who want to remain in Quebec under any circumstances.

Mr. Balducci, we believe there is a better way . . .

*From Canadian Press, May 2, 1983.
(Mr. Balducci's name has been changed.)

Preface

It's not easy being an anglophone in Quebec. French-Quebecers think that you're as passionate as a snow tire, wine stewards automatically bring you the worst vintage, and you can't even go out for a quart of milk without worrying that your family will move to Toronto.

Worst of all, *you* end up feeling guilty for two hundred years of oppression that you didn't even get a chance to enjoy. So why not leave?

Because, it's home. Because every time that you visit Toronto, or Ottawa, or Calgary you feel as foreign as if you were in Addis Ababa. The people go to bed early, they all walk in straight lines and they don't know how to *fête*. Within hours, you miss home.

You miss the chaos of the streets, the quiet of Mount Royal and the *scene* on Rue St-Denis — even if you only go there when friends are in from out-of-town. You miss the french fries in the Laurentians and the fresh corn in the Eastern Townships . . . you miss the warmth of the people, if not always the government.

You miss conversations that you *can't* eavesdrop on, and people who you don't understand. You miss the romance, the allure, and the tension of being an "oppressed minority". You never know what's going to happen next.

You're a junkie, hooked on Quebec: you can't live with it and you can't live without it. You're stuck here forever, and you don't mind a bit.

This is a book by Quebec anglos who love this province, even when they're upset with her. It's written by people who are bothered with some things that are happening here, but bored by people who constantly complain about them. It's a book for those of us who never want to leave Quebec, and those of you who've left but wish you could come back.

It's meant to remind English-Quebecers that they have much to celebrate, even if they have reason to complain. And to remind French-Quebecers that even if we are as passionless as snow tires, we've still got soul. We hope you enjoy this book too, even when you think that you shouldn't.

Because in the end, for all our differences, there's at least one thing that English- and French-Quebecers have in common these days: we're all due for a good laugh.

A nos lecteurs français: soyez assurés que ce livre n'est pas sérieux du tout. Prenez-le comme une blague amicale; ce n'est rien qu'un "joke".

To our English readers: we mean every word of it.

Josh Freed and Jon Kalina
Montreal, 1983

Thanks to Pamela Chichinskas, Evelyne Hertel, J.W. Stewart, Barbara Steinman, Fawn Duchaine, Lynette Stokes and Sherri Clarkson for their help in editing, writing, designing, conceiving and parenting this book: also for showing patience with a collection of deadline journalists who can't write anything until the last minute. Without their help The Anglo Guide to Survival in Québec *would never have survived.*

Table of Contents

A Voyage East

A Wilderness Guide to East-End Montreal

Mike Boone

For timid, uptight anglos who've never been east of the salmon counter at Waldman's, the east end represents Montreal's heart of darkness. It is the area of the city where French Quebec begins and high-speed car chases end, where the Parti Québecois and Diane Tell reign supreme and unchallenged.

It may be exciting to go to Place des Arts and laugh at Yvon Deschamps's monologues, without understanding a word he's saying. Or to sing "Gens du Pays" during St. Jean Baptiste Day in an N.D.G. park. But exploring the source of the Québecois soul requires a trip to the east end: An area of Montreal which is to the Québecois spirit what Mississippi is to the blues.

But where exactly is the east end?

As most anglophones are aware, just a few years ago Montreal was thought to end at St. Lawrence Boulevard. Only recently have we discovered a large body of inhabited land extending eastward — at least as far as St. Denis Street, perhaps even further.

Here then, is a wilderness guide to this still uncharted territory: A survival manual for the adventurous traveller, the hardy anglophone, ready at last to explore the Mysterious East.

Bon Voyage
Allo Police

PREPARING FOR THE TRIP

Before leaving, draw up a detailed itinerary of your east-end tour and leave duplicate copies with next of kin and with Alliance Quebec.

Inform relatives that if you are not heard from within a week of departure, you are either dead or dancing nude in a bar on Gouin Boulevard East. In either case, your membership to the Beaconsfield Golf Club is to be terminated.

Have your appendix removed. East-end hospitals are now as good as those in the west, but they are still *different.* The health care personnel to whom anglophones are accustomed — Jewish doctors, Filipino nurses and Greek orderlies — are not to be found in French hospitals. A precautionary appendectomy will help prevent unnecessary hospitalization in the east end.

Draw up a will. Hey, you can't be too careful. The chances of an east-end fatality are virtually nil if one avoids driving or walking, or drinking in a tavern. A carefully-worded legal document affords your loved ones a measure of security should you return to the west and announce you intend to marry a 16-year-old topless dancer.

HOW TO GET THERE

By Air: You can fly directly from Dorval, in the west island, to St. Hubert Airport, then bus in.

From downtown Montreal: The city's metro runs all the way to Honoré Beaugrand, a station so far east that it's co-administered by New Brunswick.

Surface travel, however, is more colourful and interesting: hop the 24 bus heading east on Sherbrooke and ride it to the end of the line.

A cautionary note on bus travel for the unilingual: Speak to no one. Stand near the exit so that if someone speaks to you in French, you can get off the bus.

However, if you have mastered Grade 5 French and want to try fitting in, see the section on "Riding the Bus".

WHEN TO GO

The east end is open almost all year round, except Christmas, when it goes to Fort Lauderdale, and July when it goes to Maine. Picking the best season for your visit will depend largely on your preferences in sports and recreational activities.

In scheduling your trip it is prudent to remember when *not* to visit the east end:

— The night of a provincial election;
— During police raids for bank robbers;
— The morning after the Montreal Canadiens are knocked out of the play-offs, again.

CUSTOMS AND IMMIGRATION

The east end is still technically part of Canada, so you will not require a passport, visa, visitor's permit, etc.

For identification purposes, however, it is wise to travel with a driver's licence and a medic-alert bracelet which reads: "English hospital, please".

HEALTH AND SAFETY

Contrary to what you heard from your mother, no shots are required for a visit to the east end. You *can* drink the water, although many residents prefer not to.

CURRENCY AND BANKING

The Canadian dollar is the accepted currency in the east end, for now. Banks are open regular hours, but few people use them apart from tourists. Locals prefer the "Caisse Pop".

Note: A caisse pop is not a soft drink. It is a "banking co-operative" where you bank for patriotism as well as profit. Customers are not simply "depositors", but members of a private club — like the Lion's Club — although members of this club are rarely English.

Les caisses sometimes pay the same interest rates as banks, but are much more exciting: occasionally one goes bankrupt, and you lose most of your money. The baccarat of the banking world.

Open a small account before you leave on your trip. In tight situations, flash your card. It may help.

READING MATERIAL

— *Les Nègres blancs d'Amerique,* by Pierre Vallières.
— *Bingo for Beginners.*

Contrary to popular misconception, the *Gazette* is acceptable reading matter in the east end. *Le Devoir* is not, however, read by anyone living east of Outremont; the *Globe and Mail* ought to be tucked inside a copy of *Allo Police.*

Adventurous anglos should consult *Le Journal de Montréal* before planning their itinerary. *Le Journal* will give you a complete breakdown of any east-end crime which occurred the night before, including biographies of the victims, 8 x 10 photos of the bodies, and even the address of the slaying, should you wish to visit.

Visiting *is* encouraged. In fact, *Le Journal* even includes the name and phone number of the police inspector, should you want to become part of the story. Reading the *Journal de Montréal* is a *must* if you plan to take part in tavern conversations. When you hear someone talking about a murder you have read about, just break in:

"Décapité, eh? . . . Je l'ai connu. I knew him well."

After all, who'll say you didn't?

HOLIDAYS

The east end does not celebrate St. Patrick's Day, Canada Day, Dominion Day, Victoria Day, Lord Simcoe Day or John the Baptist Day.

It does celebrate "le Fête nationale", Dollard des Ormeaux Day (formerly Victoria Day), and Canadien's Stanley Cup victories.

Banks are closed on these holidays, . . . but the taverns keep right on serving.

HOW TO GET AROUND

Foot power is your best bet. If you insist on travelling by car, hang a pair of fur dice and a Virgin Mary from your mirror. In fact, line the whole interior of the car with fur.

When driving, be mindful of a few quirks unique to east-end drivers, i.e., they drive like everyone else in Montreal.

This means:

Motorized vehicles — cars, trucks, motorcycles, hearses, etc., travel at 100 km/h in the right-hand lane. The left lane is reserved for motorists making illegal turns.

One should also be aware of how to interpret traffic signs and signals: STOP/ARRÊT or, more commonly, ARRÊT with STOP painted over, means slow down to 50 km/h to entice pedestrians off the curb.

A red light means proceed with caution, green means go, and yellow means go like hell.

Stationnement Interdit means No Parking unless you can't find any place else to park.

RIDING THE BUS

If you want to blend into the east end, *don't* head for the back of the bus. Sit right up in the front seat and talk to the driver. Unlike west-end people, who treat the driver as if he were part of the front-door mechanism, east-enders treat him as though he were a human being.

Ask him about his job, and his vacation (but don't get his name or number; you're not trying to pick him up). When you leave, wave and say "Merci, . . . bonjour"!

Don't worry. You don't have to tip.

SPORTS AND RECREATION

— Ball hockey: All year long. Pack your skates and sneakers.
— Bingo: The curling of the east end. Five dollars will buy you ten cards, a rabbit's foot and a crucifix. (Miniature elephants are extra.)

Beware. If your experience is once-a-week Bingo at the Westmount Y, don't expect to win. The elderly women of the French Bingo circuit have been playing seven nights a week for the last forty years, and are to Bingo what Gretzky is to hockey. Wear elbow pads. They play fifty cards at the same time, with both hands blurring in space. Also, God is on their side. Location: Any church, any time.

— Cycling: If you're into dangerous sports . . . try cycling east of St. Laurent. It's the white-water rafting of east-end transit.

SEPARATIST-SPOTTING

You may be worried that your east-end voyage will be marred by an encounter with a separatist. This is unlikely. The hard-core separatist is no longer indigenous to this part of town and rarely strays east of the bars on St. Denis Street. In fact, the only time most separatists venture deep into the east end is to visit their mothers at Christmas.

The separatist in the east end is easy to spot. He wears a pained, pinched expression brought on by two hundred years of oppression and the difficulty of getting a good cup of *café au lait* in this part of town.

TIME ZONES

Whether you're French or English, just remember the Montreal rule: When asking for the time, it doesn't matter what you say, so long as you point at your wrist.

ACCOMMODATIONS

Hotels and motels abound in the east end; but the traveller anxious to sample the true flavour of the neighbourhood will want to stay in a walk-up rooming house.

A comfortable, clean room can be rented for $25 to $50 a week. That will buy you a bed, clean linen, a bureau, a night table, and access to a bathroom in the hallway which you will share with a World War II vet who wanders around all day muttering about Mackenzie King and conscription, and wakes up screaming every night.

Note: "Tourist rooms" are generally not for tourists. If you still haven't got the picture, they're rented by the hour, not the day.

HANDY NUMBERS TO CARRY WITH YOU

The nearest English-speaking person during your east-end voyage is Mr. Percival Crump, 3810 Wolfe Street. Drop in anytime; he likes to entertain visitors from the mainland.

Other handy phone numbers you should carry with you:

— The Canadian Embassy
— Alliance Quebec

— Murray Hill Limousine
— Your mother

FOOD

On virtually every corner of the east end, there are restaurants which offer traditional Québecois cuisine: B-B-Q chicken, pizza, pogos, michigan red hots, packaged smoked meat, steamed hot dogs and, of course, the vegetable indigenous to the east end: Patates frites.

Like any area, the east end is not without its share of inferior eateries. There are certain clues for travellers wishing to avoid heartburn and heartbreak:

If a restaurant's menu lists something called a "hambourgeois", leave immediately.

Avoid any restaurants at which the table-top condiments do not include mustard, relish, steak sauce, vinegar in an old soft-drink bottle, ketchup, a large salt shaker and a well-thumbed copy of *Le Journal de Montréal.*

Do not eat at any establishment in which the sum of the tatoos on the cook's arm and the hickeys on the waitress's neck is less than 10.

Do not complete your trip without sampling La Poutine, the latest nouvelle cuisine delicacy which is sweeping the east end. This dish consists of french fried potatoes (overcooked in oil that has not been changed since Maurice Duplessis died), sprinkled with tiny morsels which taste vaguely like cheese curds and smothered in thick, brown gravy of sufficient viscosity to lubricate the crankshaft of a bus for 10,000 km.

Mmmmmmmmmm, good!

You will want to climax your east-end dining experience with a large slab of sugar pie — which is pecan pie, hold the pecans. Sugar pie is not among the recommended dishes of either the Dental or Diabetes Associations, but what do they know? This dish is the ideal topper to an elegant meal of La Poutine. Wash it all down with a good vintage of KIK cola. On special occasions, bring your own bottle of *Cuvée Dépanneur.*

DRINK

Of course, man does not live by food alone. While visiting the east end, the traveller will want to sample the atmosphere of the area's fabled taverns and nightclubs.

The proper beer to drink in an east-end tavern is draft, and the way to order it is by holding one, two or three fingers in the air when a waiter is nearby.

The traveller wishing to ingratiate himself with the natives may order a round of beer for a nearby table. It is inadvisable to join the patrons in their revelry, however. An unsuspecting tourist with insufficient command of French may spend a happy afternoon drinking with his new-found buddies, only to find out at closing time that he has agreed to either finance a truck hijacking, marry a spinster sister, or pitch for a softball team.

A couple of jaunts to east-end taverns should prepare the visitor for a night of bar-hopping.

The east end comes alive at midnight, offering the bon vivant a veritable cornucopia of nightlife. Whether your taste runs to adolescent strippers, country and western singers, or Elvis imitators, the east end abounds in bars and clubs which throb with the pulse of Québecois joie de vivre.

But east-end nightlife is not without peril. The wise traveller will observe a few simple rules in choosing an appropriate venue for fun and frolic:

— If there are more than twenty motorcycles parked in front of a club, do not enter.

— If the doorman asks if you are armed, say No. If he then offers you a gun, leave immediately.

— Do not tarry in clubs where men are methodically dousing the furniture with gasoline and stacking tables against the exits.

— If you find yourself in a boîte à chansons, do not attempt to lead a rousing chorus of "Lloyd George Knew My Father".

— Order nothing but beer, vodka or *le Gros Gin.* Do *not* ask for a tequila sunrise, marguerita, or other Crescent Street concoctions.

Women travelling alone in the east end are to be especially cautious. Even the most demure smile directed at the bartender can be misinterpreted; and an anglophone woman's east-end tour could turn into a nightmare of unrestrained passion for which a Westmount upbringing is poor preparation.

A note on tipping: Travellers need not tip dépanneur clerks, but gratuities are accepted and expected in most Quebec establishments, including restaurants, taverns, nightclubs and gas stations. Over-tipping is recommended for nightclub doormen — especially the big ones.

LANGUAGE

East-enders will be pleased to serve you in any language . . . as long as it is French. While your secondary education and university language training may serve as sufficient preparation for a week in Nice, your *pathetic* babbling will prove almost incomprehensible to the east-ender.

The language of the east end is *joual,* a Québecois patois which cannot be learned anywhere west of Parc Lafontaine.

≈≈≈≈≈≈≈≈≈≈≈≈≈≈≈≈≈≈≈≈≈≈≈≈≈≈≈≈≈≈≈≈≈≈≈≈

Faced with the impossibility of mastering *joual* in a short time, the traveller may prepare for a trip to the east end by learning a few indispensable phrases which should suffice on what is, essentially, an exploratory mission into foreign territory.

Herewith, the expressions you will need to know to get around the east end:

Fuck, it's cold! — Calice, il fait frais!
Fuck, it's hot! — Calice, qu'il fe chaud!
How much does this cost? — Ça coûte combien?
Where is the metro? — C'est où le métro?
Do you speak English? — Parles-tu anglais?

For a more complete guide to *joual,* see page 135.

GOING HOME

"You can't go home again", wrote Thomas Wolfe, and he'd never even been to the east end.

It would be inadvisable to fly directly out of St. Hubert Airport back to Dorval. The east-end experience is not easily shed, and direct re-immersion into Anglophone Montreal could bring on a cultural variety of the bends. You could find youself ordering "frites with gravy" at Chenoy's, or cursing foul winds, in French, at the Pointe Claire Yacht Club.

Instead, ease gently back into anglophone life. Take a slow bus down Sherbrooke Street and hop out at St. Lawrence Boulevard for a smoked meat. Read the *Gazette* over a cherry coke. Then, drop your slides off at NDG Photo and head over to the Ritz for a scotch and soda. If you're still not ready, take a room for the night. If you are leaving, remember — the last bus to Dorval leaves at midnight.

Don't tell anyone where you've been.

STOP READING THIS BOOK!

A message from the Régie

To Whom It May Concern:

Our office has made every possible attempt to stop the publication of this book. Unfortunately, this is beyond our power — for now.

However, a word of caution. *We know who you are.* Sales of this book are being closely monitored, and a list of buyers kept for future reference. Ask yourself: Are a few cheap laughs really worth the risk?

We at the Régie feel that this book is not appropriate reading material for a minority group. Leaving aside the language in which it is written, the book has an incorrect attitude, and fosters deluded feelings of equality among English-speaking residents of Quebec. It can also cause blindness.

It is *not too late* to stop reading, now. Right now! Just put the book down, immediately, then bring it down to the nearest *Office* and turn it in — along with the names of five other people you know who are reading it.

We at the Régie will be glad to replace the book with your choice of any of the following three Québec works:

— *Les Nègres blancs d'Amérique* (Pierre Vallières)
— *Ma Vie* (Maurice Duplessis)
— *La Petite histoire du Québec (version française)*

Merci de votre attention.

Yours cordially,

La Régie

Demain ne vous appartiendra pas

Les Dialogues

Josh Freed

No matter what your native tongue, you probably have a second language in common with everyone else in Quebec: franglais — a strange mix of English, French and sign language that helps you buy the paper, get directions, or get drunk.

Franglais is completely uncharted linguistic terrain, less studied than Kickapoo or Novesperanto. Yet it is the only real cement between Quebec's mosaic of language groups.

There are five basic "garden varieties" of Quebec franglais:

DIALOGUE I	DIALOGUE II
l'Anglais et le Français	*Le Franglais*

DIALOGUE I

A: Hi!
F: Bonjour.

A: I'd like a pound of coffee, please.
F: Oui, m'sieur. Régulier ou filtre?

A: Regular, please. Is it fresh?
F: Oui, m'sieur. Il vient d'arriver hier. . . . Voilà, m'sieur.

A: Thanks. How much is that, please?
F: Quatre dollars et quatre-vingt douze, m'sieur.

A: Four dollars and ninety-two cents. There you go. Thanks very much.
F: Pas de quoi, m'sieur.

A: See you tomorrow, Jean-Pierre.
F: A demain, Phil.

DIALOGUE II

A: Hi!
F: Allo.

A: Ah! Français. . . . uh . . . avez-vous de . . . to-mates?
F: Ah . . . toma-toes? . . . Oui . . . 'ow much you want?

A: Uh . . . je veux un pound.
F: Five 'undred gram . . . oui. Any'ting helse, m'sieur?

A: Uh . . . non mercy. . . . Combienne, s'il vous plaite?
F: D'at's one-tirty-tree, please, m'sieur.

A: Ah . . . un dollar et trawnt-trwah . . . oui. Here . . . uh . . . tray bien mercy.
F: You wel-comme, m'sieur.

A: Mercy. . . . Bonne jour.
F: Oui, m'sieur. I see you hagain.

DIALOGUE III
Le Francophobe

A: Hi!

F: Bonjour, m'sieur.

A: (oh, oh) Bonjour . . . uh
. . . avez-vous de . . . uh
. . . de cheese?

F: Eh?

A: De cheese . . . avez-vous?

F: Je ne comprends pas du
tout, m'sieur.

A: DE CHEESE! You know,
. . . What the hell is it called?
Uh . . . de . . . de . . . de fro
. . . de FRO-MAJ! That's it!
De fro-maj. Avez-vous?

F: Du fromage? Oui, m'sieur.
Combien-en voulez-vous?

A: Un pound, s'il vous plaite?

F: Pardon, m'sieur?

A: Un pound. UN POUND! . . .
SEIZE OUNCES!

F: Ah! Une livre. Oui, m'sieur.
Voilà, m'sieur. Ca fait unet-
quatrevingtun-puis-la-taxe-
cela-fait unetquatrevingtdixneuf, s'il vous plaît, m'sieur.

A: Uh, . . . combienne?

F: Comme j'ai dit, m'sieur. Ça
fait unetquatrevingtdixneuf,
s'il vous plaît, m'sieur.

A: Ah! One ninety-nine. Oui,
. . . uh . . . avez-vous change
pour un vingt dollars?

F: Oui, m'sieur. That's twenty
dollars minus one-ninety-
nine makes eighteen dollars
and one cent coming in
change for you, sir. . . .
Thanks for coming.

A: Taber-nacle!

DIALOGUE IV
French Like Me

A: Bonjour.

F: Bonjour.

A: Avez-vous de jam-bone?

F: De jam-bone?

A: Oui.

F: Oui . . . j'ai.

A: Quelle sorte?

F: Uh . . . je ne comprends
pas. Répétez, s'il vous plaît.

A: Uh . . . je veux de jam-bone.
Quelle sorte avez-vous?

F: Ohhh! Quelle sorte? . . .
Toutes sortes . . . et vous?

A: Excusez, je ne comprends
pas, m'sieur. Est-ce-que vous
parlez anglais?

F: Uh . . . oui . . . et vous?

A: Oui, . . . je suis anglais.

F: You are? Hey! My name's
Scotty. What can I do for
you?

A: Hey! Alright! Lemme have a
pound of ham, man.

A: No sweat.

DIALOGUE V
The Usual

A: Excusez, m'sieur, Par-don.
F: Oui, m'sieur?

A: Je veux le bus pour NDG.
F: Quoi, m'sieur? J'ai pas compris. . . . Parle-tu anglais?

A: Oui, . . . yes. Which way is the bus to NDG, please?
F: Je m'excuse. Ah don' hunnerstan'. Parle-tu français?

A: Uh . . . le bus pour NDG. Which way? Où il est?
F: Vous cherchez l'autobus? . . . Which way you go?

A: N . . . D . . . G . . . Uh . . . I can't remember what it stands for. . . . Noder Dame de . . . uh . . . It's out west somewhere. Il est dans le West.
F: L'ouest? . . . Ou l'est?

A: Le west. (points) Là!
F: Ah! L'ouest. . . . You walk one — how you say — street? Dat way, . . . den turn . . . and she's coming right by. Comprends-tu?

A: Un block là . . . et tournez . . . et l'autobus . . . , eh?
F: Oui, m'sieur. C'est exact.

A: Ah, bon . . . mercy. Uh . . . avez-vous loor, sil vous plaite?
F: Eh?

A: Loor . . . avez-vous loor? (points at wrist).
F: Ah! L'heure! Oui, m'sieur! De time is . . . uh . . . ten past tirty.

A: (looking at watch) Ah! . . . Ten-thirty.
F: Oui, m'sieur. D'ats what hi say. Ten past tirty, non?

A: Oui, . . . oui, m'sieur. Trente après dix. . . . Mercy beaucoupe, m'sieur. Mercy.
F: C'est rien, m'sieur. . . . 'Ave a nice day, eh?
A: Mercy. . . . Mercy. Bonne jour à vous, m'sieur.

Le Instant French

It's Just English in Disguise

Stephen Phizicky

Parlez-vous français?
Un peu.

Is this *you*?

If the answer is Yes, then you must be an anglophone who was born in Quebec.

Face it. If you spoke Russian as well as you speak French, you'd be in the diplomatic corps.

But because you are a Quebec-born anglophone, you are terrified of even trying to speak French. In fact, you think that you can't. Your inability to become *perfectly* bilingual has made you believe that you aren't bilingual at all.

You suffer from *Le Guilt,* hiding your French in the closet so that no one will hear how *bad* it is. You have become an immigrant in your own land.

How did this happen?

You made the mistake of going to school. There, you were taught French by instructors from France, North Africa and the West Island, i.e., anyone but Québecois. These people taught you that you would *never* speak French properly — and then proved it.

How?

With irregular verbs and imperfect tenses. With unfathomable masculine and feminine forms. With rules of agreement you would never need in talking, and mind-boggling tenses that you would never meet in life: the future anterior, le passé simple, and the pluperfect, imperfect, interior posterior.

The mind reeled; it still does. And little wonder. If you worried about things like this in English, you'd be too embarrassed to speak *that* as well.

But don't worry. We've got some good news for you. You *already* speak French; you just don't know it because it's locked up somewhere inside your mind. We're going to show you how to release it with a revolutionary new method called

Le Nouveau français

This is le solution to le guilt; le réponse to le question; le chance you've been waiting for. It ain't pretty, but it's pretty good.

THE STRATEGY

The overall rule is: Fill the air with words. As long as you're talking, there's a chance the other person is listening — maybe even understanding.

But if you're standing there mute, trying to remember how to say it *correctly,* the other person will be bored . . . and probably switch to English.

The following rules will help you fill the air with words. Not the right words, but ones that are easy to find, and close enough to get the message across. Instant French — to ensure that you always have *something* to say.

The second Rule of thumb is: If you don't know the French word, use the English one. For example, in the garage:

"Bonjour. Est-ce-que vous reparez le . . . uh . . . uh . . . uh . . . le *crankshaft*?"

Surprise! You got it right. Most French Quebecers say "crankshaft", too.

Façile, huh? Okay, now you're ready for the hard stuff.

Bon luck.

MASCULINE AND FEMININE

In a world where soup is feminine but consommé is masculine, ketchup is masculine but mustard is feminine, lettuce is feminine but cabbage is masculine, . . . face it, you haven't got a chance. Be honest. Do you every say "Mrs. Table" or "Mr. Carpet" in English?

"Le" and "la" are impossible for the anglophone to master, so why bother trying? Forget them. The rule is: use "le" for everything. Here's how it looks:

le homme
le femme
Ville LeSalle
Lechine Rapids

Easy, eh? Feminists, however, may use "la" for everything, should they prefer. It makes no difference, as long as you *only* use one. For example:

la femme
la homme
Lavesque (René)

Either way, you will be right half the time, and understood all of the time. Make it plural (les) and you'll be right all the time.

CONJUGATION DES VERBES

In le Nouveau français, there are only two tenses: the present and the past. There is no future. The "future bypass" looks after that.

The Present

The present tense is the important one — the one they make you practice in school a lot, as in:

je prends
tu prends
il prend
nous prenons
vous prenez
ils prennent

In le Nouveau français, this is called the présent compliqué. Say hello to the présent simple:

je prends*
il prends
nous prends
vous prends
ils prends

---

*There is no "tu" unless *you* want it. More about this later.

Doubtless, they'll sneer at the Académie française, but they'll understand perfectly in St. Henri de Mascouche.

The Past

Le Nouveau français uses the easy past — the one with "avoir" (to have), as in *j'ai acheté.*

Ever since high school you've been haunted by the 16 exceptions that use "être" (to be), as in *je suis allé.*

You've never been sure which verbs should "be", and which verbs should "have". This might have been a fascinating question for Jean-Paul Sartre — but not for you, especially when you're trying to learn French.

Forget the 16 exceptions. In le Nouveau français there are *no* exceptions. There are only rules. So, all past tenses are formed the simple way, as in:

> j'ai allé
> j'ai venu
> j'ai assis

It's getting easier, huh?

Now, remember "vous avez" and "nous avons"? Good. These give variety and cadence to the past. Here, then, is the entire conjugation of the past.

> j'ai allé
> il avez allé
> nous avons allé
> vous avons allé
> ils avez allé

Use "avons" and "avez" interchangeably, to taste.

The "Future Bypass"

Remember, there is no future in le Nouveau français. There is only the "future bypass". To bypass the future, you simply combine the verb you want, with the present of the verb "aller" (to go).

For example: In the present tense, "je vais" means "I am going". The verb "tuer" means "to kill". Combine them, and you have "je vais tuer", which means "I am going to kill".

Presto! You have bypassed the future.

Similarly, "Je vais vous tuer" means "I am going to kill you". [Unless you are a "tu" type person (see below), in which case use the more friendly "Je vais te tuer".]

The Subjunctive

You don't know the subjunctive in English, why bother learning it in French?

DE AND DU

What difference can it possibly make?

TU AND VOUS

In school, the rule was: It all depends on whom you're talking to. The result? You waste your life trying to figure out how you "feel" about people. Are they a "tu", or really a "vous" person?

Worrying about this can give you ulcers. In le Nouveau français, it doesn't matter *who you're talking to:* It only matters *who you are.*

The rule: Uptight, formal people should call *everyone* "vous". Informal, back-slapping types should call *everyone* "tu".

Just figure out what kind of person you are, a "tu" or a "vous" type, and you never have to worry about it again.

However, this is an important decision. Give it some thought. Hint: If you wear ties, or silk dresses, you're definitely a "vous" type. If you wear t-shirts, particularly if you wear them inside out, you're a "tu" type.

Warning to Tu People

Full-time use of "tu" is acceptable, but can be dangerous. There are times when it may pay to switch to "vous". Among them:

— a policeman, before he gives you a ticket;
— an income tax auditor, any time;
— an inspector from the language cops. In this case, it is best to call him "maître".

If you insist on using "tu" at all times, leave a will.

Warning to Vous People

Unless you are part of the Royal family, there may be two exceptions that even you can afford to make:

— your lover;
— your children.

These exceptions make for harmony in the home, and allow for very subtle communication.

For instance, if the person you share your bed with gives you a sunny smile and says "Comment *voulez-vous vos* oeufs?", you know it's not going to be a peaceful New York Times Sunday.

NEGATIVES

When in doubt, always say "non". (You probably remember *that* from your referendum ballot.)

As in English, you can always change "no" to "yes", but changing a "yes" to a "no" makes enemies.

You may recall being tortured in high school with double-barrelled negatives (ne . . . pas; ne . . . que; ne . . . jamais) — and with where to place them in the sentence.

Forget all that. The only word that counts is "pas".

The Nouveau français rule is: To make a negative, put the word "pas" in the sentence *somewhere, anywhere*. Then add "non" at the end of the phrase. This is how it works:

"Je veux pas acheter ça, non."
"Je veux pas danser, non."

Most Québecois use only the "pas". Most Parisiens swallow the "ne". The only people who use both are Quebec anglophones . . . and the people who taught them French.

QUESTIONS

Asking questions in French is easy. Look inquisitive or mystified. Say the sentence as a statement, but put a question mark at the end of it (with your emphasis):

"Vous venez ici souvent?"
"Vous voulez danser?"

This should cover most situations. If you find it hard to look inquisitive when talking on the telephone, resort to advanced Nouveau français.

The rule: Make questions by putting the phrase "est-ce-que" (pronounced S-kuh) at the start of the sentence:

"S-kuh vous venez ici souvent?"
"S-kuh vous voulez danser?"
"S-kuh vous voulez voir mes etchings?"

Façile?

ACCENTS

There are four accents in French: (ˆ); (`); (´) and (ç). If you look at your typewriter, you will probably not see any of them on it. This is a hint.

Forget accents, except for é (which sounds like "ay"). This accent is very useful as it permits us to tell the difference between a côte de boeuf (a side of beef) and être accoté (slang for "living together"). By using é you won't make the mistake of going to a French restaurant and saying:

"Garçon! I'd like to live with you."

VOCABULARY

This is the important part. It's also easy. Because French is really English in disguise.

Complicated, legal and technological words are often identical. Look at the following list — if you don't understand some of these words, then you don't speak English either.

télévision	astronaute
constitution	circonstances
gouvernement	touristes

spectacle	discrimination
passeport	inadmissible
président	observateur

The longer they are, the more they seem alike.

The rule: When searching for a French word, think fancy, then add "er".

For example, you might be thinking "begin". Elevate that to "commence" and "commencer", the correct French word, jumps into your mouth.

Or "catch" as in "catch a thief". Upgrade that to "apprehend" and you see the French word is "appréhender".

To "run" a meeting is to "preside" over it, so the verb is "présider" and the person who does it is the "président".

Other examples of how French is really English in disguise follow:

English	Fancy English	French Disguise
to hunt	chase	chasser
weak	feeble	faible
to finish	achieve	achever
glove	gauntlet	gant
thin	meagre	maigre
sheep	mutton	mouton
the same	parity, parallel	pareil
to drill	pierce	percer

to dive	plunge	plonger
to lock	bar	barrer
to climb	mount	monter
to sing	chant	chanter
to walk	promenade	promener
to free	liberate	libérer
door	portal	porte

LE NOUVEAU FRANÇAIS SPECIAL BONUS

Surprise. You can apply these rules to Spanish by adding "o" to all words. For Italian, just add "i" to everything.

Congratulations! You now speak four languages.

REVIEW

Don't forget: Fill the air with words.

When uncertain, use your hands, make a face, mumble and slur the English word with a French accent.

The key is to speak boldly. Speaking bad French boldly is better than being silent and correct.

Flaunt your Nouveau français whenever you get a chance. Sure it sounds horrible, but if you speak French badly for long enough, you *may* eventually learn to speak it correctly.

LE CATCH

Remember, now that you *speak* French, it's up to you to figure out how to understand it.

EXERCISES

1. Call a Quebec government bureaucrat and refuse to speak English. It's your right.
2. Put up an English sign, then turn yourself in to the language police (anonymously).
3. Become a member of the National Assembly.
4. Take your winter vacation in Florida, and your summer break in Maine.
5. Enroll yourself in French kindergarten.
6. Raise your child to be French-speaking. (See "Bringing Up Bébé" elsewhere in this volume.)
7. Take a French lover.
8. Leave Canada, give up your citizenship, then apply for readmission from abroad. You will then be eligible for a subsidized French course, offered only to immigrants.
9. Read corn flakes boxes.
10. Take your landlord, or your tenant, to the Rent Control Board. Go through the entire process in Nouveau français.
11. Commit a minor offence. This will get you up to two years in a French-speaking provincial jail. Caution: make sure it's not a major offence. Anything over two years will land you in an English-speaking federal jail. This would be a complete waste of time.
12. Move to Chicoutimi.

THE UNILINGUALS GO FOR A DRIVE

Prayer or Profanity?

A Guide to Cursing in Québecois

Gerry Bergeron

You've just informed the taxi-driver in your "best French" that you're not a tourist in Montreal and that this is *not* the fastest route to your destination. He responds with an incomprehensible tirade of words. The tone suggests abuse, which you expect under the circumstances. What puzzles you is a vague religious undercurrent.

Puzzle no more. This is not an exhortation to accept Jesus into your heart. You are the victim of a *joual* cursing assault.

Unlike English where the human body is considered dirty, *joual* cursing draws its material from the body of the church.

There are only two rules to remember when cursing in Quebecois:

— Know your ecclesiastic terms. Virtually any religious term can be used in swearing, if you say it right. In fact, if you *don't* intend to swear at someone, it's best to avoid religious discussion entirely.
— Any non-religious term is perfectly clean.* [For instance, while *sacré tabernacle* (sacred tabernacle) would be strong language in front of your shop steward, *c'est tout fucké* is perfectly acceptable in the presence of your mother.]

That said, here is a handy guide to a few common Québecois cusses:

_____

*exception to rule: *maudit anglais*.

†✱℅#?@♨☪!&†✱℅#?@♨☪!&†✱℅#?@♨☪!&†✱℅#?@♨☪!&†✱℅#?@♨☪!&†

FRENCH (with joual Pronunciation)	LITERAL ENGLISH TRANSLATION	EQUIVALENT MEANING
hostie (estie, or just stsie)	host; small delicate wafer representing the body of Christ. Used in communion ceremony.	son-of-a-bitch!
calvaire (kalver)	Calvary; the place where Christ was crucified.	son-of-a-bitch!
sacrifice	holy sacrifice	son-of-a-bitch!
Sacrement (sacraman)	sacrament; the Holy communion; the Body and the Blood of Christ	son-of-a-bitch!
esprit (s'pree)	the Holy Spirit; the spiritual embodiment of the Lord	sun-uv-a-gun!
tabernacle (tabarnak)	tabernacle; altar	shit!
taberouette (tabarwet)	tabernacle	shoot!
tabernouche	tabernacle	sugar!
taberslaque (tabaslack)	tabernacle	shucks!
calice (khaliss)	chalice; vessel into which holy wine is poured	fuck!
caline (khalin)	same as above	fudge!
caline de bine	same as above	fuddle-duddle!
baptême	baptism	shit!
bateau	baptism	ship!
ciboire	pyx, ciborium	geezuz!

†∗Ƶ⌁#?@⌁ʗ!&†∗Ƶ⌁#?@⌁ʗ!&†∗Ƶ⌁#?@⌁ʗ!&†∗Ƶ⌁#?@⌁ʗ!&†∗Ƶ⌁#?@⌁ʗ!&†

coq	cock	rooster
fromage	cheese	cab driver
maudit (moodzie)		damn!
merde		shit!
maudite merde		holy shit!
maudit Christ	Anti-Christ	Camille Laurin
eau bénite	holy water	holy piss!
étole	lace ceremonial garment worn by the priest	Look what the dog brought in!
saint	holy, sacred	cursed
vièrge	virgin	virgin

If you find these terms a bit raw, here are some milder ones to use when visiting your aunt:

mon dieu	my God	my God!
mon doux	my sweet	my goodness
seigneur!	saviour	Lordy!
ma foie de Jésus	my faith in Jesus	landsakes!
pour l'amour de Dieu	for the love of God	Lord love us!
fucké	fucked	broken; in a state of disrepair

LESSONS

1. Now that you've learned the glossary, perhaps you'd like to try some *joual* cursing of your own. Here's a simple rule to help you make up your own curses:

— Any religious terms, preceded by "mon" and followed by "stsie" can be used as a curse. Therefore:

mon + religious term + stsie = curse

For instance, take an innocuous term like "encensoir", which means "incense holder":

mon + encensoir + stsie = monencensoir-stsie! = you turd!

There. It's as easy as Grade 3 arithmetic.

2.   If you want to experiment with something more complex than one-liners, use the magic equation, and sprinkle in a few "de's" and "en's" before each religious term.

Here are two popular examples (honest!):

Example I

Mon hostie-de-tabernacle, m'ot crisser une calice de claque s'a guele, en sacrifice!

Literal translation: My host of the altar, I shall Christ you a chalice of a smack on the muzzle, by sacrifice!

Actual meaning: You son-of-a-bitch! I'm gonna knock your fat head off!

Example II

Hostie-de-saint-sacrement, mon p'tit calvaire, ramasse tes ciboires de claques, pi crisse ton camp, ou b'en donc, tu vas en manger une vièrge!

Literal translation: By the host of the holy sacrement, my sweet Calvary, gather up thine goblet of rubbers and Christ your camp, lest you consume the virgin!

Actual meaning: You son-of-a-bitch-of-a-son-of-a-bitch! Pick up your rubbers and beat it, or I'm gonna make you wish you'd been picked up for child-molesting!

†*%ɔ#?@ℛⓒ!&†*%ɔ#?@ℛⓒ!&†*%ɔ#?@ℛⓒ!&†*%ɔ#?@ℛⓒ!&†*%ɔ#?@ℛⓒ!&†*%ɔ#?@ℛⓒ!&†

EXERCISE

Getting the hang of it? Think you're ready to try one on your own to see if you've figured out the fine line between cussing and ecclesiastics? Okay, let's see if you can decipher the following lofty expression. Just consult the glossary, translate, and fill in the blanks.

When you're finished, turn the page upside down to check your answer.

Mon dieu! J'accepte l'hostie du Christ au sacré tabernacle et j'avoue garder l'esprit du sacré fils dans le chalice de mon coeur.

Your   translation: _____

_____

_____

_____

Actual meaning: Oh, Lord, I accept the body of Christ at the holy tabernacle and vow to revere the spirit of the holy son in the chalice of my heart. Amen.

Joining the Gentry

Elaine Shatenstein

Desperate to fit into the new Québec?

You've taken six years of French courses, hung around St. Denis Street until dawn and vacationed in Old Orchard — but you still don't feel like a "vrai Québecois".

Well, stop worrying. There's an easier way than you think to become "maître chez nous": just marry into French society — preferably high society.

By joining the gentry, you'll never again have to feel guilty about being an "oppressor". But you will have to make allowances for what you don't have in common.

UNSHARED MEMORIES

Trivial Pursuit will be out of the question — not because you have different *languages*, but because you have different *trivia*. Unshared childhoods make for unshared memories.

For instance:

— You were tucked into bed with *Grimm's Fairy Tales* and *Mother Goose.* He went to bed with *Les Contes de La Fontaine* and *Tante Lucille.*
— You remember watching Ed Sullivan; he recalls *Les Beaux Dimanches.*
— You solved crimes with Nancy Drew and the Hardy Boys; he explored with Tintin and Bob Morane.
— You struggled through the PSBGM's French classes; he worked on his Greek at a private "collège classique".

MEETING THE FAMILY

A Kiss is Not a Kiss

The well-known French custom of a kiss on both cheeks comes into play here. But don't try to impress them by rushing forward with lips puckered. The greeting kiss is a symbolic ritual that in no way involves the mouth. Let others make the first move — they'll approach with head angled so that only your opposite cheeks make actual contact. When in doubt, shake hands.

Learning Your Name

Insist that they pronounce it properly, even if it is Ramsbottom. Be ready to explain its origins, but don't go into too much detail. If they are having trouble, translate it and introduce yourself as Cul-de-bélier (Bottom-of-the-ram).

Learning His Name

If Emile is the scion of one of the best families, he's apt to have up to eight Christian names (as in Joseph-Marc-Yves-Léon-Emile-Michel-Alain-François). Concentrate on just one, like Emile, and teach it to your family. Don't worry about them calling him Emily by mistake. Even after you've been with him for years, your relatives will persist in asking "How's Pierre?"

GENEALOGY

Resist the impulse to trace your roots — his family tree will make yours look like a sapling, especially if you're a recent immigrant.

— His ancestors sailed with Jacques Cartier; yours came here in a cargo hold in 1919.
— His great-grandfather tended Verlaine on the battlefields of Europe; yours tended goats in the Urals.
— His grandmother marched to Ottawa with Thérèse Casgrain; yours fed the kids and did piece-work at home.
— His uncle ran the Ministry of Education; yours ran the corner store after dropping out in Grade 9.
— His family has been speaking English for 200 years; yours learned it in 1925.

MARRIAGE

If you don't want to offend anyone, you'll have to have two wedding ceremonies — or hire simultaneous translators. Your best bet is to simply live together, thereby uniting your two families in shame and disappointment.

HOME LIFE

Along with the usual adjustments of co-habitation, special allowances must be made to accommodate your two solitudes:

Meals

Get used to drinking real French wine with dinner and having salad *after* the main course. He'll have to adapt to breakfasts that feature food.

Space

Two daily papers at least, not to mention a double set of books and magazines. You'll need a spare room.

TV and Radio

Two of each is ideal; otherwise, work out a schedule whereby you trade him hockey in French for the Expos in English.

Quarrels

Whatever is spoken at home, remember that in the heat of battle, you'll both revert to your respective native tongues and not understand a word the other is saying. This is just as well — there will be less to regret later.

Sex

Along with music, this is one of the few areas in life where language and class pose no barrier. Make the most of it.

BY GOD, SHIRLEY AND I AREN'T
GOING ANYWHERE! WE THINK
OF OURSELVES AS BOTH GOOD
CANADIANS AND KAY-BEC-WAH.
HOW COULD WE DEPRIVE OUR
KIDS OF THE TREMENDOUS'
CULTURAL PRIVILEGES HERE?
YOU KNOW, THE CURVED
STAIRCASES AND ALL THAT...

SO, THE COMPANY IS PAYING
FOR MY CRASH COURSE AT
BERLITZ. AND SHIRLEY IS
TAKING CLASSES TWICE
A WEEK AT THE SHOPPING
CENTER IN QUÉBEC
UPHOLSTERY. WE FEEL
THAT WE DO BELONG HERE
AND CAN CONTRIBUTE.

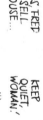

BESIDES WE
CAN'T SELL
THE HOUSE...

KEEP
QUIET,
WOMAN!

AISLIN #

Bringing Up Bébé

Why Does My Child Sound Like a French Garage Mechanic?

Victor Dabby and David Sherman

You've done your best to be part of French Quebec. With Radio-Canada blaring in the background, you sip your Pernod on ice and peruse the day's *La Presse* with quiet satisfaction.

Into your living room walks your 8-year-old bilingual *wunderkind* — the living symbol of your commitment.

To attone for the countless sins of a dozen generations of anglo oppressors, you've sent your child to French-speaking "garderies" and the finest French schools.

All is very "normale", as they say in PQ circles. That is, until the day she walks into your living room and hits you with: "Ça m'tente plus de parler Anglais, papa. J'veux être comme tout le monde."

You don't understand a word she says, so you just smile and nod, as always. But later, your francophone neighbour translates for you and you get the message loud and clear:

Your daughter is giving up the English language. She wants to be like everyone else: "normale".

Can this really be?   Or are you just a character in a PQ minister's wet dreams?

You always wanted your child to learn French, but it's one thing to *speak* French, and quite another to *be* French. You quickly enroll your daughter in a three week English-immersion course in Vermont.

DANGER SIGNS

Here is a ten-point litmus test for identifying the latent linguistic turncoat in your family:

1. Calls you "Papa", and thinks "Dad" is an oatmeal cookie.
2. Sings "Gens du Pays", instead of "Happy Birthday".
3. Demands fish on Fridays, hambourgeois on Saturdays, and soupe aux pois during the rest of the week.
4. Frowns whenever you speak English; corrects your pronunciation whenever you speak French.
5. Translates all government mail for you. Answers the phone and the door in French.
6. When her/his French friends come over, they laugh and point at you. You just smile and nod, feeling like an immigrant in your own house.
7. Visible boredom if anybody other than René Lecavalier is doing the play-by-play on the Saturday night hockey game.
8. Extensive use of such phrases as: *Je veux to faire do-do. Buy me a beau cadeau. What jour is it? I'm making a gros ca-ca. Let's take the autobus to the parc.*
9. Glazed eyes when you mention Spiderman (and you haven't a clue as to the identities of Capitaine Québec or Goldorak).
10. Inability to identify Mr. Rogers or Big Bird.

FIGHTING BACK

If your children flunk the litmus test, perhaps it is time to consider fighting back . . . before they're old enough to turn you in to the language cops.

The following hints for "anglifying" your children have been excerpted from a Quebec handbook designed to assist cabinet ministers in surreptitiously teaching English to their children.

1. Hide the *Tintin* books and replace them with *Mother Goose*.
2. Strike out the French side of cereal boxes and other packages.
3. Slide a cassette player under their pillows at night and play tapes like "Old MacDonald Had a Farm" and "English in Ten Easy Lesson". Other choices: The Constitution, the BNA Act, and "This Land Was Made For You and Me".
4. When they watch French TV, tell them to turn it off and do their homework. When they watch English TV, serve them milk and cookies.
5. When they start dating, subsidize their English dates; not their French ones.
6. Lead your children in a rousing chorus of "It's a Long Way to Tipperary" in the shower each morning. Actually, it's not as far to Tipperary as they think. That's where you're sending them to boarding school if their English doesn't improve.

BRINGING UP BÉBÉ

Despite the perils of assimilation, it is important to equip your children for life in the new Quebec. Following is a brief guide for bringing up your bilingual bébé to be *maître chez lui.*

Naming Your Bébé

A wrong choice could cripple your loved one for life. Be safe. Stay away from the obviously anglo (Percival, Winthrop, Harold, Marjorie, Cassandra).

The clever parent will either make up an exotic name that makes no sense in either language, or else simply consult the Bible. Biblical names are very chic in Quebec these days, and they roll off the tongue equally well in both English and French.

For example:

Luke—Luc
Samuel—Sam-yew-ell
Michael—Me-shell
Matthew—Mat-you
Paul—Pol
Rachael—Ra-shell
Sarah—Sa-rah
Miriam—Mir-yam

The New Testament is always safe. Some Old Testament names (Ephraim, Nehemiah, Nebuchadnezzar, and Jehosaphat, for example), don't quite work in Quebec.

Also whatever you call your children, keep in mind the hyphens that lie ahead under Quebec's new name law . . . or you might end up with a great-granddaughter named:

Ariel Fung-McCormick-Papadopolous-Beaulieu

No-No Names for Anglos

René, Camille, Pierre-Marc, Jacques-Yvan, Marc-André, Gérald, Claude, Rodrigue, Raynald, Pauline, Bernard, Jean-François, Clément, Jacques, Grégoire.

Le Babysitter

Quebec has one of the highest unemployment rates in the western hemisphere; take advantage of it.

Drop in at the local supermarket and check the bulletin board for an unemployed babysitter.

Just look under the Ph.D. column (there'll be lots), and choose one of those with a doctorate in French. For balance pick one that also has a minor in English Literature.

LE GARDERIE

Choosing a Garderie

Remember, your choice of a daycare centre says who you are and where you want your child to go in the new Quebec. The anglo parent who wants a "semi-normale" child should be wary.

First, check out the name of the garderie. If it's called "Garderie libre", drop in first and make sure the children aren't separated into cells.

If it's a *garderie populaire*, find out if your child will come home singing the "Internationale", in French.

If it's a *garderie à but non-lucratif*, make sure your child packs his/her own milk and cookies.

And if it's a *garderie privée*, look out. You'll pay through the nose.

Implicating Yourself

Now that you've chosen a garderie, be prepared to work in the collective spirit of Quebec. You haven't just signed up for daycare; you've become a member of an extended family. This means working for a garderie committee.

Don't be intimidated by the committees' authoritative sounding names. The more important they sound, the less they do. However, certain committees are to be avoided at all costs. They include:

— Comité de transport. This means picking up a dozen kids every morning at the crack of dawn.
— Comité de nourriture. This means cooking regularly for three dozen hungry four-year-olds.
— Comité d'entretien. This means washing floors and patching the holes in the fleur-de-lys that flies over the doorway.

Generally, it is best to stay away from all of the above unless you have a strong desire for work. Recommended is the Comité pedagogique et administratif, where members enter into endless discourses on theories of child-rearing and education.

During the monthly meeting, anglo parents are advised to remain silent and nod sagely as points are raised. If pressed for an opinion, memorize the phrase:

On a besoin de plus de consultation.

Le Bébétalk

If your children are exposed to a garderie during their first year, you may find that their babytalk differs markedly from that of your nieces and nephews in English daycare.

Do not be alarmed; this, too, is "normale". Here is a brief glossary of babytalk for understanding your Québecois bébé.

un la-la — a horsie
un lo-lo — a hot milk before bed
un bo-bo — a boo-boo, a cut or bruise
un do-do — a nap
un doo-doo — a blanket
un tu-tu — a teddy bear
bébé lala — a crybaby
un pipi — a pee-pee
un ca-ca — messy in both official languages

LE SCHOOL

After le garderie comes school, the big league. Ignore the widespread misinformation about the subject.

Through a number of loopholes, English-language schooling is available to the children of anyone who:

— can prove their family is related to Louis Riel;
— is a direct descendant of Jacques Cartier, or at least married into the family;
— can prove they are fabulously wealthy, and will take their money elsewhere if their child does not get into an English school;
— can list the 16 PQ "martyrs" who went down to defeat in the 16 by-elections; and give 10 reasons why Bill 101 is the most humane piece of legislation since the *Magna Carta*;
— has a father who was a classmate of a government minister when they studied at Oxford, Yale, Harvard or any other school not in Quebec or France;
— knows the sexual proclivities of PQ government ministers, and has a videotape to prove it.

If you fulfill the last criterion, the question of educating your children in Quebec is academic. The government will probably reward you with a foreign posting to a Quebec mini-embassy in Paris, New York or Belgium. Your children can then attend the same exclusive schools that government ministers send their children to and learn the same language as they do — English.

EPILOGUE

Your children should thank you one day for all your trouble, but probably won't. If you're lucky, they will grow up bilingual, and be able to ignore you equally well in either language.

How Many Anglos Does It Take...

Q: How many anglophones does it take to screw in a light bulb?
A: One — to call a French electrician.

Q: How many anglos does it take to cook a good meal?
A: None. It's impossible for an anglo to cook a good meal.

Q: How many people are there in a anglophone orgy?
A: One or two.

Q: How many anglos does it take to make love?
A: Four. Two in the bed and two underneath to shake the bed.

Q: How many aspirins does an anglo ("têtes-carrées") take for a head-ache?
A: Four — one for each corner.

IT WAS A SHATTERING EXPERIENCE WHEN I REALIZED I COULDN'T COMMUNICATE IN MY USUAL GLIB MANNER...

UM... HAVEN'T WE MET APRES?... ER... BEFORE??
AW, PHOOEY....

NOW, I'M NO LONGER THE LIFE OF THE PARTY.... INSTEAD, I'M REDUCED TO FOCUSING ON INANIMATE OBJECTS.....

GOSH, WHAT AN INTERESTING DOOR KNOB.

AND IN ORDER TO CONVERSE IN PUBLIC, I DISGUISE MYSELF...

HOWDY!

HOW MUCH FOR THAT CHURCH?

SO, WHY DON'T I LEAVE?

I DID TRY TORONTO WHERE EVERYONE IS UNILINGUAL. I FOUND IT VERY BORING...

WHAT DO YOU DO?
I ASKED YOU FIRST.
YOU SURE LOOK SEXY IN THAT LEISURE SUIT....
HAVE I SHOWED YOU MY MONEY?
YAWN..
WASN'T THAT A GOOD CHEESE SANDWICH?

POUSSES-TOIE!!!

I PREFER MONTREAL WHERE I CAN IMAGINE WHAT PEOPLE ARE SAYING.... IT'S SO MUCH MORE ROMANTIC....

Carioli '83

Functioning as a Fonctionnaire

On Becoming One of the Six English-Language Civil Servants in Quebec

Josh Freed

Congratulations. The Quebec government has adopted an affirmative-action program to get anglophones into the civil service.

You are now one of *six* English-speaking civil servants in the province — thus trebling the quota.

You have become a *fonctionnaire,* part of Quebec's new elite — and you're hoping to stay there. How do you fit into your new world? Just follow these easy instructions:

RULE 1:

While you must speak French at all times, *do not* try to *be* French. You aren't French, and your colleagues will know it. Pretending you are will make them think you're a phony.

RULE 2:

Do not be English, either. All English people are seen as colonizers and exploiters. If you are one of them your colleagues will resent you.

What does that leave? Simple.

Become an ethnic.

Anglophones are hopelessly out of fashion these days, but ethnics are still quite acceptable — even "in". Unlike anglos, ethnics are seen as part of the Quebec mosaic: Les communautés culturelles. Moreover, most civil servants are anxious to embrace ethnics — as long as they act cute, wear colourful national costumes and don't demand services or signs in their own language.

How can *you* become a cute ethnic?

Well, if you are already ethnic your job will be easy. If not, you'll have to find the *hidden ethnic* inside of you. Somewhere in your past, there's probably a strain of Italian, Jewish, Scottish or Serbo-Croation. Find it and cultivate it.

Search out your roots. Find out who your great-great-great-great grandparents were. Find out who *you* are.

ETHNIC LIKE ME

Once you have chosen a suitable "ethnic self", learn to play the part well. Be colourful, be exotic. You have a stereotype to live up to; don't disappoint your co-workers.

Wear your national costume. Sing tunes in your native tongue. Eat strange foods like baklava or spumoni.

If at all possible, try to be a member of an "oppressed minority" — especially one that has been oppressed by the English.

Talk about your oppression and your lost culture. If you're Irish, tell them you want independence for the North. If you are Greek, say the Turks tried to throw you into the sea.

Jewish? Tell them that your language — Yiddish — is dying. Just don't mention that it's the Jews who are killing it, by switching to Hebrew.

Caution: Under no circumstances should you complain about Quebec's own policy toward immigrants. It is good to be an oppressed minority — as long as the oppression happened someplace else.

SOME SAMPLE IDENTITIES

Scottish:

This is an easy one. If you really *are* a Scot, you know that the Scots were even bigger exploiters here than the English — but many of your colleagues probably won't. Why tell?

They probably think that the Scots are colourful, highland dancers, who speak Gaelic. Don't disappoint them. Bring in your family album with pictures of your uncle wearing a kilt (don't mention that in reality he's a bank president).

Dress the part yourself. Wear plaid skirts, ruffled blouses and a tam.

At some levels of government you may find that your department has an annual "Talent Night" party at Christmas. Bring your bagpipes.

If you don't play the pipes, just read them a poem by Robert Burns. A good choice would be *Ode to a Mouse:*

> "O wee, sleekit, cow'rin', tim'rous beastie,
> O what a panic's in thy breastie, . . . "

This will amuse them greatly.

Jewish:

Civil servants go to the movies and many are fond of Woody Allen. Study him carefully.

Dress in ill-fitting clothes, be artsy and emotional, and have a good repertoire of existential jokes. Be bittersweet. This will be expected of you.

However, it is wise to avoid old stereotypes. For instance, don't offer to lend money to anyone in the office.

North American Indian:

Lay a guilt trip on them.

This was *your* land first, and they know it. Indians are the only people on earth who can make French-Quebecers feel guilty. Do so.

They may have been exploited by the English, but *you* were exploited by the English *and* the French. Don't let them forget it.

Tell them that most of your family was wiped out by Dollard at Hochelaga. Dress in ceremonial garments that have historical significance to them — like the jacket you ripped during the QPP salmon-fishing raid at Restigouche two years ago.

Old Stock:

If all else fails and you have to admit that you're dyed-in-the-wool English — play the part well. Even a purebred anglo can be an exotic "ethnic", if she knows how to live up to her stereotype.

Look like something out of *Wuthering Heights.* (Most civil servants have read it.) Have masses of curls and tangles in your hair. Be mysterious and dangerous.

The French Lieutenant's look is quite chic as well. Wear a black robe and hood. Don't let anyone see your face.

FITTING IN

Before reporting for work, keep in mind that Quebec civil servants are as hard-working as any civil servants in Canada. But they do have different cultural traditions from bureaucrats in say, Victoria, or Queen's Park.

Following are some general hints to help you blend into your new landscape — whether in Montreal or Quebec City.

General Hints:

— Smoke Gitane cigarettes, and let them cling to your lip when you talk.
— Trade in your Cutlass for a Renault 5. If you're executive level, make it a Peugot. Remember — Ford Escorts are the mark of a federalist.
— Carry *Le Devoir* at all times. Leave stray copies of *Le Nouvel Observateur*, *Le Monde*, *Libération* and *Canard Enchainé* littering your desk. Ask your colleagues if they have read the "witty" piece by Foglia in *La Presse* that morning. They will be impressed by the mere fact that you understand him.
— *Never* refer to Bill 101. In your new world, it is "La Charte de la langue française". Refer to it as simply "La Charte" (as in *Magna Carta*).
— If you went to l'Université de Montréal, mention it. If you went to McGill, and it comes up, say that you took part in the McGill Français march.
— As you are a civil servant, they will assume that you voted YES in the referendum. Don't spoil it.
— Tell them that you hate Toronto, Calgary, Edmonton, and especially Ottawa — though at least the latter is close to Hull.
— Talk about your vacation a lot, the one you had and

the one you're going to have. Tell them you spend summers in Maine and winters in Florida or Mexico. The Mexicans all think you're one of "Los Tabernaclos".
— Become active in the union; this will confuse them since they won't expect it from an "anglais". In fact, become the union rep for the office. This will baffle them completely.
— *Never* be arrogant. There's nothing worse than a lippy anglo.

Regarding working hours — the usual Canadian Civil Service Code applies: It's okay to leave early, but if you plan to leave late, then you'd better have a damn good excuse.

Food

This is an important area of study in your new milieu. The French appreciate good food; civil servants more than most.

— *Don't* pack a box lunch.
— *Do* have a good selection of red wines on the tip of your tongue. (Not Quebec wines — only anglos drink those.)
— Learn to appreciate the two-hour-plus lunch; it is a well-honed government tradition. Drinking is practically mandatory, but none of that "four-martini-and-a-cab" stuff you picked up on St. James Street. Your new colleagues will walk back in a leisurely fashion to let the food digest. Wine is fine, so long as it's French. If you must have beer, make it Miller.
— If it's a "working lunch", and you work in Montreal — impress your colleagues by calling La Pâtisserie Belge before they do.
— In Quebec City, order your quiche from Kerhulu.

Fêtes:

— Get to know the birthday (fête) of *everyone* in the office. This can be an important event in a fonctionnaire's day. More often than not you'll take up a contribution and take the person out for lunch — where you will sit at a long table and sing "C'est à ton tour". (*Not* "Happy Birthday".)

— The most important fête of the year is in October. Mark it on your calendar. This is the day that the Nouveau Beaujolais arrives. Your office will probably order 15 bottles, and take a very long lunch. Don't be a spoilsport — join the fun.

Other dates to remember:
— the day the lobsters arrive from the Îles de la Madeleine (La Fête du homard);
— the day the shrimp arrive from Matane;
— the day the oysters arrive from Malpeque.

Stock up for each of them. Recipes will be on the agenda for the next week.

DRESS

Don't look plain. Montreal is known as the best-dressed city in North America — and it's not because of NDG.

Women:

Be exciting. Cashmere, tweeds and pearls are all out. Don't fall into their stereotype of the drab, old English librarian.

Have your hair done — regularly. Wear eye make-up, nail polish and jewellery. Construction boots are out. Even the most independent women have a subtle sexuality here; the French don't even have a term for Ms.

It's good to show tears occasionally, too, so they don't take you for the passionless iceberg they think you are.

Practice some gentle flirting during lunch hour.

Men:

Don't look like a stockbroker — or even a bureaucrat. You are a *fonctionnaire* — but a fonctionnaire with flair!

Let your hair grow (a bit). Start a beard or a moustache. Drop the tie and wear a silk scarf, a safari jacket — or even a jean jacket if you're in the lower echelons. Leather is always in.

Throw on some cologne, too. Get a nice leather purse to string over your arm. It's considered sexy, not weird.

PERSONAL RELATIONSHIPS DURING OFF HOURS

Be emotional. They think all anglos are cold and reserved. Tell them how you *feel.* Tell them about your relationships, especially with the opposite sex. Tell them about your mother. To them, you are an "étranger", a foreigner, and they will be curious about your "social customs" and mating habits.

Learn to "bec" in Québec. You will notice that your new colleagues don't just shake hands; they often kiss each other on both cheeks. This is a "bec". Take part — it's fun. However, if you are female, watch out for the passionate ones who kiss and grab. Kiss, but kiss carefully.

If you go to office parties, be prepared. At anglo parties we drink and talk quietly. At French parties they dance and have fun. If you want to leave, plan on taking at least 45 minutes to do so. The French say "au revoir" — and they mean it. They'll see you again at the cloakroom, at the door, at the foot of the stairs, and at your car. Saying "good-bye" isn't just a salutation, it's a process.

Send "thank-you" notes whenever possible. This is considered terribly "English", in an "ethnic" kind of way. The day after a party or a nice lunch, drop them a note. They will find it

"SPEAK FRENCH ENGLISH DOGS!"

"OF COURSE IT'S DIFFICULT FOR OUTSIDERS TO GRASP THE SUBTLE COMPLEXITIES OF THE SITUATION HERE IN QUÉBEC" quaint and "charmingly English" — as long as it is written in French.

LOSING YOUR LANGUAGE

Under no circumstances should you speak English at the office. Even if there is a fellow anglo working with you, converse in French; your colleagues will be impressed.

If you must speak English, be discreet about it. Think about it as you would about picking your nose, i.e., don't do it in public.

Carry a portable phone and conduct all English business from the bathroom. If you do get an English-speaking call, tell others it was from outside the province; preferably somewhere in the U.S.A.

Tell your co-workers that you love Quebec, and that you love French — so much so that you're losing your English vocabulary. This will give your colleagues a secret satisfaction that they will never express.

Eventually, closet federalists in the office will reveal themselves to you. They will whisper to you in English, saying things like "They're killing the economy. . . . The money is all leaving".

You will be able to spot these federalists before they approach you: They are the only people in the office who have not had a promotion since 1976. It is best to avoid them entirely, at least until the Liberals are back in power.

SPECIAL REFUGEE SECTION

Hundreds of thousands of you have left; few have returned. You have fled as close as Hawkesbury and as far as Hong Kong in your search for "STOP" signs and a good English-speaking school board.

You are the "car people", an endless orange line of U-Hauls vanishing down the 401 — leaving us alone and abandoned.

This section is for you. The least you can do is read it.

VENDRE
931-3066

Only $1,000 Can Feed & Clothe This Anglophone Family for a Week

Douglas McClaren was a successful VP of Marketing when his head office suddenly moved to Toronto, without him. He and his wife, Wendy, were left behind, *alone and unilingual,* in Quebec.

The family is forced to live on U.I.C., a small trust fund, and a stock portfolio showing *almost no growth* this quarter. Their children, Timmy, 10, and Kimberley, 14, have almost *no disposable income.*

The McClarens need your help!

- Douglas's Audi is three years old
- Kimberley's ballet class is due for renewal
- Wendy is forced to wear last year's wardrobe

Timmy desperately needs to be seen by an orthodontist, while Kimberley will soon be of college age. What then? Will she be forced to go to a French university because her father cannot afford tuition in an American school?

HOW CAN I HELP?

Your small donation can help return their life to normal. For only $1,000 a week you can adopt this charming Westmount family and show them that SOMEONE CARES.

Or, if you prefer, you can make a *small donation* that will still make a difference to their shattered lives. For instance:

- Only $3,500 will pay gas and tolls to the cottage for an entire year
- Only $1,500 will send Timmy to Tennis Camp to improve his *badly underdeveloped* forehand
- Only $2,000 will keep Kimberley out of group therapy and maintain her private sessions

WHERE DO I WRITE?

Easy. Your $1,000 a week can be sent to the McClarens care of: *Hard Times in the First World* (address below). Or, should you prefer, your money can be deposited directly into Douglas's self-administered RRSP.

BUT CAN I BE SURE MY MONEY WILL ACCOMPLISH ITS GOAL?

Absolutely. As soon as they cash your first cheque, the McClarens will send you a personal letter, IN ENGLISH. Or, if you prefer, they will make a video-tape (VHS or BETA)

- See Kimberley do UNDERWATER BALLET
- Watch Timmy at DRESSAGE!

For an extra $5,000, the cleaning woman will write as well

PLEASE. Help the McClarens smile for the first time this quarter!

Won't you help...

FOR DETAILS ON HOW TO **ADOPT AN ANGLO**
FILL IN THIS COUPON:

Name: . . . .
Address: . . . .
Income (disposable): . . . .
Ethnic Origin: [ ] Franco [ ] Anglo [ ] Allo
I prefer to help: [ ] Someone in the financial community only
                     [ ] Someone whose head office has moved
                     [ ] Your choice

Send $5.00 for our publication: *Hard Times in the First World*
c/o *Anglo Foster Family Association, 1976 Montreal Street*
Toronto, English Canada

Letters Home

Montreal, 1983

Dear Refugee:

Surprised to receive a letter in English from Québec? Did you really think we had all left town or that Westmount and Pointe Claire had disappeared? Pas du tout. We're still here, some of us, and we were wondering about you and your life out there in Canada. We know it's a "big, cold and cheerful country," but there's certainly more to it than that.

Just a few questions for you:
Is it true that you only speak to ex-Montrealers?
Do you really have to go to sleep early, even on weekends?
What's it like to feel like part of the majority again?
Are the Rockies that big?
Who's the Prime Minister?

Please write and tell us about your adopted country. Can you live a Montréal life in Toronto? Ottawa? Vancouver? . . . New York?

We miss you, but we don't know if you miss us. You never write.

What's the matter . . . Your arm is broken?

Josh and Jon

The Nation's Capital, 1983

Dear Josh and Jon:

I've been in Ottawa for two years now, but I'll never be an Ottawer . . . or Ottawaite . . . or Ottawatonian, or whatever it is that they call themselves. Inside, I'm still a Montrealer -- a stranded exile, surviving on care packages from a life I can't leave behind.

You ask if I can lead a Montreal life in Ottawa. Well, to start with, on the all-important gastronomic front there are some grave deficiencies around here. For instance -- no fresh coffee anywhere in town. This means friends and relatives visiting us from Montreal find themselves transporting 10 kgs of frozen Moka Java lovingly wrapped in plastic.

Solving the liquor problem is a bit easier, after all, Hull is right next door. There, as in the rest of the world, wines are divided into Burgundy, Beaujolais, French, Italian, etc., etc. In Ottawa we have two categories of wine: "Ontario" and the "Rest of the World."

When I'm finished at the Liquor Board, I can stop at a dépanneur, buy a cold beer and drink it straight from the bottle. Just for the thrill!

My answer to the smoked meat question is that I've given it up . . . the stuff here isn't edible. I hear, though, from some Montreal die-hards, that you can order a "medium" straight from Schwartz's and have it bussed in by Voyageur (as long as you buy your sandwich a seat and arrange to have it met at the station).

There is, of course, more to city life than food and drink . . . namely nocturnal entertainment (though one sometimes wishes the nocturne could endure beyond 1 a.m.). The answer to this is, once again, Hull. The line-up of Ottawers outside "Tabasco's" on Hull's main drag is so long you'd almost think you were at the latest disco in Montreal. Almost. It may not be exactly Tijuana, but the bars and streets of Hull, Aylmer, Chelsea and other border towns are at least open 'till 3 a.m. I don't go often, but it makes me feel better knowing they're there.

As for politics, I still pay more attention to Premier Levesque than to Premier whateverhisnameis. I get The Gazette, Le Devoir and I tune my radio and TV to the local branch plants of French CKAC and TVA.

But let's set one thing straight: the idea that Ottawa is a bilingual city is a myth. I came from a place where children HAVE TO go to French school, unless they have the right papers and pedigree; now I live in a city where your child CANNOT go to French school UNLESS he/she has the right papers, pedigree, etc.

Some things I will never adjust to . . . among them the soullessness of Ottawa houses. No matter how large the house it invariably has a dark dungeon-like kitchen and a closet for a bathroom. A friend of mine has said that if architecture is the expression of values then you'd have to say that people in Ottawa don't like to eat or shit.

Yet there is one thing above all that is missing here: the parade, the panoply of people who make their way down Montreal streets. Every lunch hour is a festival, every corner a surprise: you can walk the streets for sheer amusement.

In Ottawa, the streets are a means of going places. Bureaucrats relax in shirtsleeves and ties, pot-bellied tourists are everywhere, toting three kids and a string of cameras like they had just stepped out of Mad Magazine. It's just not the same.

There is only one day a year when Ottawa acquires a brief sense of Montreal's street life: July 1. Then the streets are closed, and bandshells opened. There's music, food and tens of thousands of people flooding the streets, couples arm-in-arm, perhaps even necking.

It is a bit too orderly, a bit too safe, but still . . . for a brief while you can close your eyes and almost imagine you were on St-Denis Street . . . back home again.

And then the conductor steps up to the stage, and the band starts to play: "O, Canada."

Karl Nerenberg

•   •   •

New York, N.Y., 1983

Dear Josh and Jon:

Miss Montreal? How can I miss anything when I'm in New York? Doesn't this city have everything -- every purchasable perversion, every imagined desire?

Take that bookstore near my house. I went into it the other day and asked the clerk for a title. He momentarily removed his Walkman, looked at me with disgust and said "Don't you realize that we only carry books about Ireland here!"

Don't be the last Anglo on the 40I . . .

MONTREAL ESTATES
A Home Away From Home

MONTREAL ESTATES lets you bring the best of Montreal with you, *wherever* you go.

Our Montreal-style communities are located in six major Canadian cities . . . complete with a whole new neighbourhood of ex-Montrealers who'll help you feel right at home.

From Toronto to Vancouver, you'll find all the things you loved back home. . . . and more. You'll wake up each morning to freshly-ground Van Houtte's coffee, and a dozen bagels from the new "bagel factory" just a block away from home.

Your new home will feature *outside wooden staircases* and all the latest Montreal features . . . including *unfluoridated water* and even *space heaters*. From your front window, you'll have a great view of the **MONTREAL ESTATES** slope, topped with a small neon cross — where, yes, you *can* walk on the grass.

At **MONTREAL ESTATES**, *everything* is just like home. In fact, for purists, we'll even make it *difficult* for your child to go to school.

Make the move you've wanted to make since 1976. Pretty soon you'll be so happy in your new community, you won't miss Montreal in the least. In fact, you won't even know you've left.

MONTREAL ESTATES

. . . THE BEST OF MONTREAL WITHOUT THE BOTHER OF BEING THERE

And then there is the very large pet store in the Village. It deals exclusively with the sale and servicing of one particularly obscure breed of dog -- the Akidas. If you need guard dogs for your Japanese castle, this is the place to be.

How can I even think of Montreal when there is an entire block of twenty stores that sell only buttons and beads, when there are six thousand restaurants and one hundred museums within walking distance of my house. For those of a spiritual bent, there is the American Bible Association's glass and marble library which houses "half a million books: but only one title . . ."

Miss Montreal? Okay, I admit it, I do miss a few things about Montreal -- more than a few in fact.

I miss a banking system that works, the wide open spaces of an empty sidewalk and the "u" in colour. I miss seeing the same person twice -- ever.

I miss not having to line up for just about everything: a pay phone, buying a newspaper, even the one spot on the curb where you can cross the street without stepping in a mud puddle.

I miss knowing people who are something more than what they do or how much they make. I miss CBC radio, friends, the Van Horne Shopping Centre, a subway that doesn't offend just about every orifice of the body, and a city where you don't have to be vastly wealthy to get either sick or rent a studio apartment. I miss a geographical landscape where I have a past.

Ah, yes, I could go on and on, but my Akidas are charging around my one-room apartment anxious for their walk. I guess I'll go to my favourite Thai restaurant again tonight and read a good Irish book. . .

                    Ron Blumer

            ●   ●   ●

                        Toronto, English Canada, 1983

Dear Josh and Jon:

People here are always saying that Toronto has loosened up because of all the ethnics who have arrived. What they don't say is that one of the most important of these has been ex-Montrealers.

In the last ten years, Montreal has been slowly growing in the belly of Toronto. The Brown Derby Restaurant is here

Les Nirenberg

and Ruby Foo's is on the way. The Montreal Bistro on Church
Street serves "Ben's smoked meat," and there are occasional
"frite" wagons on the streets, complete with Quebec licence
plates (you don't even see that in Montreal anymore).

St. Hubert B-B-Q now has an outlet somewhere in Scarborough and -- be still my throbbing gall bladder! -- there
is even an honest-to-goodness Montreal bagel factory here
now.

Yes, up in the wilds of Bathurst Street, the owner --
a Mr. David Finklestein -- told me in broken English and
Yiddish, how he came to Toronto via Tashkent and Israel
JUST to make Montreal-style bagels for Torontonians. His
cousin from Montreal helped him build the wood oven . . . so
they could make the real thing, not Toronto's traditional
"electric bagel."

Yet despite this, there is much missing. There is no
Laurier B-B-Q, no Pine's Pizza, no beer in groceries . . .
and no Schwartz's. Ditto for the Orange Julep, Wilensky's
and steamies on the Main. And you still can't get a Montreal-
style steak here, without laying two Toronto steaks on top
of each other -- and quadrupling the Montreal price.

And it's not just the food that I miss; it's the life-
style too. People here are strangely interested in "how
much" you make, and "what" you are. They say things like:
"I'm a United Empire Loyalist. What are you?"

In this city you don't dare call anyone after 9 p.m. or
drop in unannounced. In Montreal, I used to leap onto my
friends' galleries and say, "I'm here!" In Toronto, if I
leap on their galleries and say "I'm here!", they say "I'm
busy . . . but what are you doing a week next Thursday?"

It is easy to be alone in this city . . . especially in a crowd. In Montreal, there are TWO solitudes, in Toronto, there are two million.

There is more that I miss. I miss the tension and adrenalin rush of driving on the Decarie expressway, never knowing if I will get off alive.

I miss the squealing tires, the jaywalking, and people who don't wait politely at the corner, like soldiers, waiting for the light to turn green.

Here, in Toronto, people make right turns on red lights -- a practice that would cut the population of Quebec in half if put in practice.

I even miss the Montreal buses -- especially the Ste-Catherine Street drivers and their bilingual call:
        "Bish-up, Bishop! Moun-tain, de la Montagne!
         Cres-cent, Crescent! Ghee, Guy!"

There are, of course, things I don't miss. I don't miss bank robbers, arsonists, and kinky MLAs. I don't miss Jean Drapeau or the public libraries Montreal doesn't have.

In closing, drop me a line saying how things are:
        Are the light bulbs still working on Mount Royal cross?
        Are the streets still icy in winter and full of pot-holes in summer?
        Are Bicycle Bob, Frank Hanley, the Great Antonio and Kid Oblay still alive and well?
        And most importantly, do the girls still smile back at you on the downtown streets?

Please forward my usual order: ten pounds of smoked meat, two Wilensky's Specials and a jar of Mrs. Whyte's Pickles. But from now on . . . you can skip the bagels.

                        Your ever-hungry friend,
                        Les Nirenberg

●   ●   ●

                        Vancouver, Pacific Ocean, 1983

Dear Josh and Jon:

Like every city in Canada, we have our Montreal-style B-B-Q chicken, our Montreal steamies and even a Montreal restaurant with Montreal-style fries. But there is much we do not have, and never will.

In no particular order, these are the things I miss:
1) The press of humanity: street life. 3 a.m. traffic

jams on Ste-Catherine Street, even on a Monday.

2) The "ethnic" feel: three German shops here and they call the street Robsonstrasse. Hunky Bill's "pierogis" are about as exotic as it gets.

3) Post-winter potholes: it's hard to live without seasons. Vancouver's perpetual spring, sometimes rainy, sometimes just damp, is pretty -- but relentlessly green.

4) Bank robbers and gangsters: it's one thing to go for a bare dip in the chilly Pacific, another to take a deep six in the St. Lawrence wearing cement boots. There is an absence of danger here.

5) Bread made with fewer than 14 fabulous grains, six of them sprouted. Also, crust -- or even a baker who has heard of it.

6) The pace: it is hard to adjust to a city where every-one is laid back, where rolfing and iridiology, aromatherapy and reflexiology are all taken seriously. Vancouver is a city waiting for a collective heart attack.

Overall, when I talk to other Montreal refugees, we usually start off recalling the good food. But ultimately, we find that what we miss is our youth, measured out in shoestring fries. Vancouver may prolong youth indefinitely, but it doesn't give it back.

And of course, Leonard Cohen doesn't even _pretend_ to live here.

Eleanor Wachtel

•   •   •

Car Wars

How to Cross a Montreal Street...
and Live

In New York you can be mugged if you don't know the rules. In Bogota, they'll take the rings off your fingers, and in New Delhi, they'll try to sell you cheap reproductions of the Taj Mahal. But in Montreal, if you don't watch out you'll never even make it across the street. So, if you've left town for more than ten days, consider yourself vulnerable and read this guide.

Test Question: (works equally well for drivers and pedestrians) What do you do when encountering a red light?

If you answered "Stop and wait for the green," you've indeed lost your street smarts and are in danger of extreme bodily harm when attempting to cross a Montreal street.

Remember! In no other city in North America (or possibly the world) is it thought necessary to post signs reading WAIT FOR GREEN LIGHT.

KNOW YOUR NICHE

Are you:
Pedestrian 1: The (Most) Law-Abiding Pedestrian
Behaviour: Disregards colour of light but waits for lighter traffic. Looks at traffic when crossing. Will use cross-walk if convenient. (Problem: there are few cross-walks.)
Fatality rate: highest in North America.

Pedestrian 2: Average Pedestrian
Behaviour: Crosses either on red or green. Will cross moderate to heavy traffic. Will take notice of traffic if hit.

Thinks that the term "cross-walk" has religious connotation. Does not respond to term "jaywalk".

Fatality rate: beyond measure.

Type 1

Type 3

Pedestrian 3: Kamikaze

Behaviour: Prefers crossing dark streets on rainy nights wearing black clothes. Never looks at traffic. Happiest crossing in front of trucks and buses. This pedestrian, if highly skilled, can actually "bring down" a moving vehicle, forcing it off the road and perhaps (highest marks) into a second vehicle.

Only known predator: Quebec school bus.

Fatality rate: lowest in North America.

Discouraged? Think it's best to stay in Ottawa and skate to work? Buck up, a true Montrealer never forgets (Je me souviens). Start with something basic like crossing the street with your eyes closed. Good luck and bon voyage.

For every refugee who wishes he'd never left Quebec, there is another who has no regrets. *You* are this person.

Sure, the paranoid fears that drove you out of the province haven't materialized, and you now suspect they never will. But still, you're not looking back. You've made your peace with Moose Jaw, or Medicine Hat, or wherever it is you've settled.

True, Portage and Main isn't quite St. Catherine and Peel. And you sometimes wish you could get a bottle of wine that didn't come from Kelowna, B.C. But what the heck, things could be worse.

There's really only one thing troubling you — your children. Like every parent, you watch them growing up and worry about the day they'll start to ask those embarassing questions. Especially that one terrible question that every refugee parent will eventually have to face: "Mommy, why did we leave Quebec"?

You know that you'll want to say something that will scare your child from ever returning — and leaving you alone in Medicine Hat. But the truth just isn't scary enough. What to do?

Easy. Just reach up to your bookshelf for your *Anglo Survival Guide* and turn to the following page of the book. Dim the lights, lower your voice and read your child the "Refugee Ghost Story"; the blood-curdling tale of the last of the Anglophones. It bears little relation to reality, apart from the fact that it was sort of what you were thinking at the time you left.

And if you read it to your children often enough, they may even believe it.

The Diary of Ian Frank

A Ghost Story for Refugee Children

Jon Kalina

Monday, 15 December 1984

THE ARREST

Call me Ian.

I heard a knock on the door. Outside, through my small dormer window, I could see just a few square feet of slushy Montreal street and the back end of an old Renault 5 with its motor running.

Oh, shit. A Renault 5, the car the Americans viciously called merely *Le Car*, was *Le Car* favoured by La Police. Le worst type of La Police . . . the Language Police.

But how could the tongue cops know un Anglais lived in the small room above Le Dépanneur Poupon? Even my tiny window was disguised behind the Bière d'Epinette sign.

The sound of feet coming up the stairs . . . the sneaky tread of Wallabees . . . the preferred footwear of the tongue cops. My life had finally hit the fan.

"Open up, monsieur", a gravelly voice said, "it is known that you're in dere".

It was over. He was speaking English. That meant they weren't here for a language misdemeanor . . . no slip of the subjunctive, no misplaced adjective or mistaken gender . . . I was being busted on a language felony!

The door splintered and they were in the room, all three of them singing as they always did, "C'est à ton tour . . .". "Well, well, Messieurs Noun, Verb and Predicate", I said to myself as they hustled me down the stairs. It was to be my last joke for a long time. They hadn't bothered with identification, but the big, quiet one let his jacket flap open . . . just enough to see the Petit Robert nuzzled up near his armpit.

JAIL

Day 1

I lay on a dirty cot. I didn't know the day or the time. All I knew was that the tongue cops had me locked up in the basement of some building on the abandoned McGill campus.

They came in. This time it started friendly.

"Ah oui, monsieur, we know you are Québecois. Of course, everybody nowadays is, ha, ha. But what kind of Québecois, eh, monsieur? You are a pure wool Québecois? Or maybe a mixture? Perhaps you are Nouveau Québecois? Of course, we will hold none of this against you. But we must know the truth".

"But maybe", said the thin one with wire rim glasses who insisted I call him 'Doctor', "maybe he is an immigrant, eh? Or maybe", he spat, "a bilingue?"

The friendly, fat one looked hurt. "Oh, no", he said, "we have no real reason to doubt the monsieur. But he understands that we are only doing our jobs. After all, we are all family men, . . . ha, ha".

Then it started in earnest. First the dialogues:

"Où est papa?"
"Au jardin avec maman."
"Bonjour?"
". . . lundi."
"Comment va?"
". . . mardi."

I survived. Then came dictation, vocabulaire, and the killer — explication du texte.

I knew I'd fail. I'd always fail. I broke out into a cold sweat. I dirtied my shorts.

Day 3

I woke up thinking of escape. Where could I go? All of my friends were either assimilated or worse, in Cornwall. I couldn't go to Cornwall . . . I had promised my mother on her deathbed that I wouldn't go.

Toronto was out of the question, too, . . . that road hadn't been used in years. Now the border was an impenetrable mass of hot dog stands and asbestos heaps. As for America . . . the Americans didn't want *les anglais* anymore than anyone else did. There had been yacht loads of Quebec anglophones adrift for months in the turbid waters of Lake Champlain because they had been refused entry into the States and were unwilling to return home to be "re-educated".

Maybe I could find the Resistance. Brave anglos who had refused to assimilate. They called themselves the ELO — the English Liberation Organization. But how would I ever find them?

Suddenly, the wretched notes of "Gens du Pays" came blaring out of hidden speakers in my cell. Again. God, how I hated that song! I was beginning to hear it in my sleep.

Day 4

I lay on my back trying to conjugate "falloir". I had the crazy idea that if I could remember all the endings in the *passé simple* I would become invisible and I could just walk out of this stinking prison a free man.

Would it ever stop? What did they have against us? Why were we English always persecuted? Me, a former CEGEP teacher, holed up like a weasel in a dirty storeroom above a filthy dépanneur. Startled every time a Renault 5 backfired on the street. Only going out at night, in the spring-time . . . and then only to go to the bathroom outside like a free man . . . like a French man. Why couldn't I have been born French? Why? Why?

Day 5

I woke up with a splitting headache and the taste of maple syrup in my mouth. Brushing the tourtière crumbs off my pants, I surveyed my cell. Something had changed. Had there always been varnished wood on the walls? And those black velvet scenes of Le Vieux Montréal. Sure they were beautiful — but had they been there yesterday? I couldn't remember.

I lay back and closed my eyes. Suddenly, with a nasty burst of clarity, I remembered. Three tongue troopers and myself in the interrogation room. The three of them playing spoons and me wired up to a cauldron of maple syrup. The torture machine they called *Our Lady*. I had been "sugared off".

I opened my eyes and tried to see the black velvet paintings for the schlock they really were . . . I had it for a moment, then as the soothing tones of "Gens du Pays" came floating into the cell, I lost it. After all what did art matter? Or education? Did it really matter what language you spoke, . . . or your children? Who needed to understand everything anyway?

Day 6

I woke up with the sun in my face, feeling wonderful and humming a favourite tune of mine, "Gens du Pays", when my three best friends in the whole world came in.

"Jean, my boy, we have some good news for you".

I smiled. "A new copy of *Allo Police*"?

"No", said Doc, "better than that. Today you are well, my friend. You are well enough to go and take your place in our society".

"You mean", I said, not believing my ears, "C'est à mon tour"?

"Oui, c'est à ton tour . . . ".

And we all sang our favourite song.

"LOOK AL, I'M MAD AT QUEBEC TOO...BUT MOVING OUR HEAD OFFICE?"

THE GUARDIAN ANGLOS

Not every anglo dreams of moving to Toronto. There is a small group of English-speaking stalwarts who will always remain, to keep anglo fires burning.

Undaunted by the flight of countless classmates, steadfast in the wake of fleeing insurance companies, ready to grapple with an endless horde of unilingual parking tickets, they are the Guardian Anglos — a resolute band of die-hards as rooted to Quebec soil as the maples on Mount Royal and the potholes in the streets.

From whence did they spring? What strange forced nurtured them? It is time their true story was told.

This section is for them — to honour the past they had, to make up the past they didn't.

La Petite Histoire du Québec

(*Version Anglaise*)

Nick Auf der Maur

From the discovery of New France to the 1981 Referendum, all of Quebec history is a lie based on a single fallacy: that the British actually wanted to own Quebec. In fact, nothing could be further from the truth. The British already had a surplus of colonies in the sunny Caribbean and took little interest in the Canadian icebox later dismissed by Voltaire as nothing more than "quelques arpents de neige".

The truth of the matter is that the British spent three hundred years trying to dump Quebec onto the French, with the French all the while stubbornly refusing to take it back. The real history of Quebec is the story of British agents working continuously, first in New France and after, in the guise of Quebec nationalists, to free Britain from this unwanted yoke. Here, for the first time, is their incredible story.

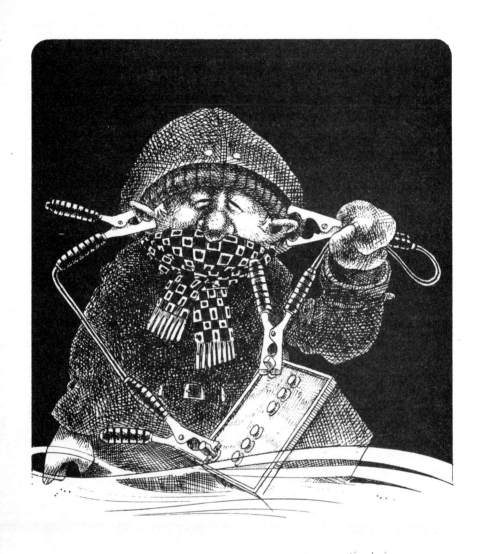

WAS JACQUES CARTIER ENGLISH?

No — but he might as well have been, since the British were behind him every league of the way.

Contrary to currently accepted history, Cartier was not the first European to set foot in New France; he was only the first one who chose to stay. This bleak chunk of frozen tundra had been an open secret among sailors for years.

Eric the Red spent one long weekend here, then scurried back to Greenland. John Cabot took one look and left. British sailors regularly passed by Quebec, dismissing it as not worth "dropping anchor".

In truth, British generals were secretly hoping that France would stumble upon Quebec and consequently expend dollars and valuable troops setting up a colony. But after years of waiting, the British, worried that France would never find it, decided to help them out.

The unsung hero of Cartier's voyage was a black African named Uriah Urdoho. He was hired on because he spoke several African dialects. Cartier thought he would be able to communicate with any savages in the New World. Unknown to Cartier, Urdoho was in fact, a British agent sent along to make sure Cartier found the correct route.

By all accounts, Cartier was a good fellow, but a lousy navigator. He didn't like the cold, and hadn't even bothered to pack an overcoat — so he had a natural predilection for steering the ship toward the south, aimed somewhere between Maine and Florida. Fortunately, Urdoho was there.

In his memoirs, later published in London, Urdoho recounts how, time and again, he wrestled the steering wheel

Did he take a wrong turn?

from Cartier's shivering hands. Shouting "That way, mon capitaine, that way!" he was eventually able to put the ship back on
its northern course. Again.

Thus Cartier discovered New France, rather than Old
Orchard.

THE ORIGINS OF CANADA

Urdoho was quite the prankster. His fluent Spanish en-
abled him to confide to Spanish crewmen that he was taking

Cartier to a land where there was *nada mas caca* ("nothing but shit"), a popular Spanish vulgarity at the time.

When speaking among themselves, the crew would jokingly refer to their destination as "caca nada". Thus, when Cartier sailed into the Gulf of the St. Lawrence, Urdoho mockingly cried out: "CACA-NADA!" — a term Cartier thought to be the native name for the newly discovered land.

Remarkably, contemporary etymologists have completely ignored Urdoho's memoirs when trying to pinpoint the presumably Indian origin of the word "Canada".

THE EARLY COUREURS DE BOIS

Once the British were comfortably settled in New England, they desperately wanted the French to stay pre-occupied in New France. But the French were having a devil of a time with the wretched colony, rarely straying out of Hochelaga.

The British, with their vast experience at empire-building and colonialism, decided to surreptitiously help out. Secretly, they sent in a steady stream of British agents and entrepreneurs to help the province prosper just enough to keep the French interested.

For example, the first coureur de bois was the famous 18th-century British highwayman, Dick Turpin, who had been caught and faced the noose. Instead, the British offered Turpin a deal — the chance to emigrate to Australia if he secretly helped the French colony develop the fur trade. When Turpin agreed, he was dumped on the shores of the St. Lawrence, and given a cover story about having escaped from Britain.

In England, Turpin's prowess as a highwayman had earned him the nickname of "the road runner".

On Turpin's arrival in New France, a French garrison commander commented, "You won't be able to run the roads and highways here, Turpin. There are no roads".

To which Turpin drily retorted: "Then I'll have to run the woods, won't I"?

Thus the métier of coureurs de bois was born.

BENEDICT ARNOLD

The American Revolution offered the British their best chance of unloading their unwanted Quebec burden. The English got one of their most trusted agents, Benedict Arnold, to convince the Americans to launch an attack on the Quebec colony.

When Arnold and his American troops set out to capture British-held Quebec, the French became alarmed; they, of course, desperately wanted the British to remain stuck with Quebec. French agents managed to sabotage Arnold's expedition by tampering with his food supplies.

On crossing into British-controlled Quebec, Arnold discovered that his pack mules were not carrying mutton, potatoes, flour, and the like as planned. Instead, they were carrying only eggs. Within days, his troops grew sick of scrambled eggs, fried eggs, and even omelettes, so Arnold ordered his chefs to create any concoction that would mask their taste.

His troops contemptuously referred to these efforts as "Benedict's eggs".

Because of this food supply problem, Arnold's troops became demoralized and the whole expedition was abandoned after a few pathetic skirmishes. A French Montreal newspaper trumpeted that the battle had been won because of "les oeufs à la bénédict", and it soon became a sought-after dish: Eggs Benedict.

Following this failure, Arnold talked Benjamin Franklin into starting up a French newspaper — *La Gazette* — to whip up French support for the American Revolution.

When this didn't work, Arnold convinced Franklin to transform *La Gazette* into an English newspaper, thinking this might make the inhabitants anti-English. This scheme was more successful and the policy is still in effect today.

LES CONQUÊTES

The 18th century saw a Britain terrified that France would abandon its colony in Quebec and look instead for the decent British colonies in the sunny south. To keep France convinced of Quebec's value, the British mounted a psychological war. They pretended they desperately wanted Quebec so that the French would want it too. To maintain this facade, the British were forced to make periodic attacks on the French colony; through this skirmishing they actually mistakenly captured Quebec once in the early 1700s. It took the British three years to give it back. On the whole, Britain's plan to protect her southern colonies worked well; the French were kept away from Florida until the mid-twentieth century.

THE PLAINS OF ABRAHAM

In 1759, with war again raging everywhere between France and England, the British knew it would look suspicious if they didn't engage the French in North America. They placed the expedition in the hands of a thirty-two-year-old, inexperienced general, James Wolfe, and gave him strict orders: "Put up a good fight . . . but lose." Wolfe devised a clever theatrical strategy. He would choose an impossible attack-route: Arriving by boat on the St. Lawrence river then scaling   the unassailable walls of the fortress of Quebec, thus guaranteeing defeat and dumping Quebec with France for good. But Wolfe's glorious defeat was snapped from the jaws of victory by Montcalm who brilliantly out-manoeuvred Wolfe and surrendered — a stroke of genius that got the colony off France's hands once and for all.

The Lee Harvey Oswald of 1759?

However, Montcalm apparently knew too much for his own good and he paid the price for that knowledge at the hands of the French double agents. Autopsies performed at the time raised questions that linger even today. Who masterminded the French strategy on the Plains of Abraham? Why did Wolfe and Montcalm — the only men who knew the truth of the two country's counter-strategies — both die? Were the bullets that killed them fired from the same gun? Was Montcalm the Lee Harvey Oswald of 1759?

The full story behind the Quebec conspiracy of 1759 may never be known but the result was there for the world to see: Britain placed under the yoke of New France for two hundred years of oppression.

BUILDING A FRENCH QUEBEC

After the Conquest, the British found themselves saddled with a Quebec they did not want. Throughout the long, cold years of occupation they diligently tried to preserve the French characteristics of Quebec — in a desperate attempt to get the French to take it back.

Thus, The Quebec Act of 1774 was passed, guaranteeing the use of the French language and freedom of the Catholic religion — more rights than the Catholics enjoyed in England at the time.

In fact, British francization attempts actually laid the cornerstone for such modern legislation as Bill 22 and Bill 101.

Although it is little known, the English governor, William Craig, had a profound influence on Quebec speech patterns. His contribution was similar to that of the 16th-century Spanish king who had a speech impediment — a slight lisp.

Just as the English strove to speak the "King's English", the Spanish believed in the King's Spanish. And so the courtiers, noblemen and ladies all imitated the King's speech pattern, establishing the mode for "proper speech" which still exists today — Castillian Spanish, which bears a slight, lisping quality.

Governor Craig also had a slight speech impediment which, together with the English accent he tried to hide, caused him to speak a peculiar kind of French.

For example, he had difficulty pronouncing the word "cheval" (horse) which came out as "joual".

Rural inhabitants were much taken with what they believed to be a fashionable mode of speech, and it was rapidly taken up and still continues today as modern "Joual".

The priests, however, were displeased with what they viewed as a "punk" version of the language. In an effort to stop its spread, they issued edicts from the pulpit warning against speaking like Governor Craig. In particular, they warned against his faulty pronunciation of church articles, such as saying "tabernak" for tabernacle, and "collis" for chalice, etc.

Although these words were rarely used by ordinary people on a day-to-day basis, they took to uttering them under their breath, as a way of expressing their admiration for Governor Craig, and showing which way their loyalties lay.

MODERN TIMES

Separatism — The English Disease?

From this new historical perspective, it is finally easy to make sense of modern Quebec politics.

What, for instance, is Quebec separatism if not another British-inspired ploy: a scheme to help Canada rid herself of the grim French wasteland she inherited from Britain? Who is René Lévesque if not a pawn in the real battle between England and France over which country would be saddled with Quebec?

It was Britain that launched Lévesque's meteoric rise during a Liberal election campaign in the early 1960s. Lévesque had been hastily telling colleagues that "We've got to make a damn revolution here". But a key British agent, Eric Kierans knew that for the plan to succeed it had to be camouflaged.

Repeatedly, he warned Lévesque: "Yes, yes, René, but we have to keep it quiet, we have to go tranquillement. It must be a *quiet* revolution".

In the following two decades, British agents fostered the rise of nationalism, urging innocent Quebecers on at every turn. Take de Gaulle's famous "Vive le Québec libre" speech, which fired the beginnings of the PQ cause. Whose interests did de Gaulle really represent? With whom was he allied during the war? For whom did he really work — if not MI-5 — British Intelligence?

Is it any coincidence that the name of the heir apparent to the British throne, Charles, Prince of Wales, translates in French to Charles de Gaulle?

A top British agent?

Did he deliberately sabotage separatism?

Laurin to the Rescue

During all the key events of the following years, British agents and provocateurs lurked everywhere, fanning the nationalist coals: Stanley Gray, the mastermind of the McGill Français march, Nigel Hamer, the sixth man (MI-5) in the FLQ crisis, Henry Milner, the true architect of sovereignty-association.

Much of the PQ itself was, of course, part of the British team: crack British agent David Payne, WASP establishment figure Kevin Drummond, Jacques Yvan-Morin (recruited in his formative Oxford years), and Jacques Parizeau, the London School of Economics professor who brought the expression "By jove!" to a whole generation of Francophones.

All were part of the elite British squad, fostering their dream of a separate Quebec, forever cut adrift from British or Canadian dependence; a barren, bankrupt iceberg that would eventually have only one way to turn — France!

Only a small group of men stood in the way of the British plan — the remaining French agents working in Canada. These men knew that if Quebec separated, it would eventually become a North American Chad, tied to French purse strings forever. They knew that there was only one way to block the British plot — by destroying the PQ.

The names of these brave French agents are well-known — men like Gilles Gregoire and Claude Charron, Marcel Léger and above all, Camille Laurin — men who bravely infiltrated the nationalist movement and sacrificed all to discredit separatism.

They knew that if France was to rid herself of its unwanted burden for all time, Quebec could have only one future: it must remain "une province commes les autres", tied forever to a united Canada (the Commonwealth of nations).

And thanks largely to the heroic efforts of Laurin and his group, it is a dream that finally seems within grasp.

An English-Speaking Street Guide to French Montreal

English	French
Noder Dame	Notre-Dame
Jeerward	Girouard
Curbs	Querbes (Kairb)
Deleppy	De l'Epée (de Laypay)
Dilooth	Duluth (Du Lutte)
Raychul	Rachael (Rash el)
Mary Ann	Marie-Anne
Henry Julian	Henri-Julien (Onree Shulien)
Esplanaid	Esplanade
Saint Veeaytur	Saint-Viateur
I-Burville	Iberville (Eeberville)
Saint Lawrence	St-Laurent
Da Bull-yawn	Du Bullion (Dew Boolyanh)
Gene Talon	Jean-Talon
Henry Berassa	Henri-Bourassa
City Hall	Hôtel de Ville
Chrisopher Columbus	Christophe-Colomb
Pappy-no	Papineau
St. Dennis (pre 1960)	St-Denis (St. Deh-nee)
St. Denny (post 1960)	
Lack-a-dee	l'Acadie
Saint Urban	Saint-Urbain
Berry	Berri
Veedur	Vitre
Coat Saint Luke	Cote St-Luc
Coat Vertwo	Côte-Vertu
Gene Manse	Jeanne-Mance
Ville a Marde	Ville Emard
Long-gale	Longueuil
Dick Harry	Décarie
Pie Nine	Pie IX (Pee Neuf)
Clossay	Closse
Gwen	Gouin

MARTYRED STREETS

Was	Is	Year of Death
Maplewood	Edouard Montpetit	1968
Craig	Saint Antoine	1976
Macgregor	Docteur Penfield	1978
Burnside, Western	de Maisonneuve	1966
City Hall	Hôtel de Ville	1895
Bellingham	Vincent d'Indy	1972
Ontario Ave.	Ave du Musée	1975
Fletcher's Field	Parc Jeanne-Mance	*
Town of Mount Royal	Ville Mont Royal	1982
Wilder	Antonine Maillet	1982

*The names Fletcher's Field and Parc Jeanne Mance, although popularly used, are both incorrect. The official name is Mount Royal Park (since 1874). In the English community it came to be called Fletcher's Field in 1875, when an officer by the name of Fletcher began holding military drills there.

TURNCOAT STREETS

Was	Is
Pine	Avenue des Pins
Queen Mary	Avenue de la Reine-Marie
Park Avenue	Avenue du Parc
Mountain	Rue de la Montagne
St. James	Rue St-Jacques
St. Peter	Rue St-Pierre

NAMES YOU'LL SEE CIRCA 1990

Is	Will Be
Bishop	L'Evèque
Crescent	Croissant
Greenfield Park	Parc Champs Vert
Atwater	A L'Eau
Westmount	Ouestmont
Kirkland	Terre de Kirk
Dr. Penfield	Docteur Champs Stylo
Hutchison	Hotchicken
Van Horne	Van Houtte
Westminster	Ministre de l'Ouest
Somerled	L'Eté Plomb
Victoria	Dollard des Ormeaux
Wolfe	Attila the Hun
the 401	Autoroute 101
West Island	Scarborough East, Ont.

"HEY, GUS! IT'S ONE OF THOSE LANGUAGE COPS..."

Paradise Lost

The Montreal Star
Mile End Station
The Van Horne Mansion
The 17 Streetcar to Belmont Park
The Engineer's Club
Rockhead's Paradise
Her Majesty's Theatre (now Place des Arts)
The Bistro
Le Palais D'or Dancing
Chicken Coop
The Esquire Showbar
Dominion Park (now Catelli's)
Lumpkin's Ice Cream Parlour
Dinty Moore's (now Howard Johnson's)
Northeastern Cafe
Dominion's (now Provigo)
Montreal Royals
Montreal Maroons
Montreal Alouettes
The Montreal Herald
The Alexander dump
Rachael Market
Smilin' Jack's Deli
The Auditorium
El-Morocco Night Club
Morgan's (now La Baie)
The Seven Steps (now L'Arc-en-ciel —
    prior to Bill 101 — The Rainbow)
The Bus to "Nowhere"†
King Edward Park Race Track
King's Park Race Track
Dorval Race Track
Mount Royal Race Track
Kempton Park Race Track
Eddie (Kid Baker) the "Bookie"
    (now Loto Quebec)
Bonaventure Station
Slitkins & Slotkins
Miss Montreal Diner
The Scandinavian
Honey Bee
The Swiss Hut
Elmer's Dairy
The Boiler Room
The New Penelope
The Downbeat

Montreal Heat, Light & Power (now Hydro
    Quebec)
Mount Royal Arena
Hoot-Hoot Ice Cream Parlour
The First and Last Chance Tavern
The Stork Club
The Back Door Coffee House (now McGill's
    Bronfman Building)
Drury's Steakhouse
Verdun Pavilion
Child's Restaurant (now a MacDonalds)
The Colossium Ice Skating Rink
Woodhall
Victoriatown or Goose Village
    (demolished for the Autostade, now a
    landing strip)
Golden Square Mile (now Calgary)
The 65 Bus
Black Marias††
Shapps
The Gaiety Theatre (now Theatre du Nouveau
    Monde)
Lindy's Cheesecake
Craig Terminus
Manoir Ste-Rose
The Empress (Cinema V)
The New Yorker (formerly the Verdi,
    the Canada, now for sale)
The Princess (Le Parisien)
The Capitol (Swenson's)
The Regent (Le Beaver)
The Hollywood (L'Amour)
The Van Horne (for sale)
The System
The Midway (I'Eve)
Starland Theatre
Crystal Palace (Le Cristal)
The Savoy
The Lido
The Snowdon (for sale)
Laurentian Hotel
Queen's Hotel
Windsor Hotel
Royal Embassy Hotel
Garland Terminus
312 Berger Street (ask for Denise)†††

---

†   City of Montreal bus labelled "Nowhere", that took passengers on an all-night excursion
     around town, destination unknown. Popular with young couples who had no car to smooch
     in, it was Montreal's version of a "Streetcar Named Desire". Price: two bus tickets.
††   Horse-driven caleche that picked up the tipsy and dropped them off at home. Waiting wives
     pronounced sentence.
††† Famed Montreal brothel, popular with soldiers during World War II.

R.I.P.

Drummond
Millar
McLearon
Cartierville
Crawford Park
De Roberval High
Lasalle High
Sarah Maxwell
Tetreaultville
William Trenholme
Strathearn
Merton
Westbrook
Bannantyne
Kensington
Montreal East
Riverside
Rosedale
Strathcona
Surrey Gardens
Connaught
Elmgrove

R.I.P.

High School of Montreal
Logan
Monklands High
Victoria
Wentworth High
Ahuntsic
Alfred Joyce
Baron Byng High
Dorval Gardens
Dunton High
Morison
Roxboro
Royal Vale High
Sir Arthur Currie
Devonshire
Herbert Symonds
Iona Avenue
Peace Centennial
Royal Arthur
Russell
Stonecroft
Lachine Rapids

Diehards

Orange julep
Y.M.C.A.
Piazza Tomasso
Dilallo Burger Original 1929
Murrays Restaurants
Holt Renfrew
Wilensky's
The Bagel Factory
Beauty's
Ogilvy

Mazurka
Schwartz's
Toe Blake Tavern
Ritz Carlton
Metro News
Thistle Club Curling
M.A.A.A.
Royal Montreal Curling Club
Frank Hanley

Why do you stay in Quebec?
        "My mother won't let me leave."
        Donna Steinberg, author of *I Lost It All in Montreal*

THE UNILINGUALS GO SHOPPING

Walking Backward

A Unilingual Tour of Downtown Montreal

Kathryn O'Hara

Are you:

— over fifty and hopelessly unilingual?
— too old to move to Toronto, but too young to settle in Miami?

Wouldn't you like to take a nice walk in Montreal — the way it used to be — in English?

If you long for those halcyon times come walk with the Guardian Anglos and relive the days:

— when French was not the only factor;
— when change was something small you carried in your pocket;
— when happiness was a well-skipped rink.

Put on your tartan blinders — see Ogilvy's, see St. James's, see Sir John A's statue — see precious little else.

GUARANTEED PURE ENGLISH!
English streets, English structures, English Saints,
English Squares (Tait Carray)

WHAT TO WEAR

Sensible clothing. Any item carrying the following labels is recommended: Aquascutum, AirStep, McGregor Happy Foot, Pringles, Supp-hose. In bad weather, wear Eddie Bauer. Above all, look neat.

WHAT TO BRING

— Ogilvy's shopping bag (tartan type);
— an umbrella;
— a flask of Johnny Walker Red.

PREPARATION

Say "Good morning, nice day". Say it several times. Say it loud. Walk tall.

———

The tour starts at **Windsor Station** (Gare Ween Soar). This is no ordinary train terminal. It housed the head offices of the CPR, a company directly responsible for Confederation. The first train left here in 1889 for Boston. Don't you wish it still did?

Read the plaque in honour of Sir William Cornelius Van Horne. His office was upstairs. He quashed Louis Riel's uprising by sending troops on his trains. Where is Van Horne now that we need him? He is a shopping centre and a bagel bakery.

Turn and leave through the brass-framed doors under stone porticos. Those of you who haven't set foot in these parts since 1976 may want to reconsider at this point. The next train back leaves in two hours. You could have a nice meal and a drink at the Alouette Room in the station. Except that it isn't there anymore.

On leaving Windsor Station you are immediately face to face with **St. George's Anglican**. It graced the western edge of **Dominion Square** before anything else did, and still does. Thank heaven for small blessings.

At the southern entrance of Dominion Square you'll encounter your first monument: **The Cenotaph**. Put on your poppy. Pause. Take off your poppy.

Nearby is the statue of **Sir John A. Macdonald**, alleged father of Confederation. Open your flask, take a little snort for Sir John A. Close flask.

You are now at **Dorchester Boulevard**. Risk life and limb to cross this street. Observe the statue of **Robbie Burns** gazing on the once splendid Edwardian facade of the **Windsor Hotel**. A wee dram here for auld lang syne.

In the distance, the corinthian columns of the still imposing **Sun Life** building are visible. Once the largest skyscraper in the Commonwealth, it is now abandoned.

Look down: Sir Winston Churchill stored Britain's securities in the basement vaults of the Sun Life building during WWII. Still impregnable. A sip for Sir Winston.

Look up: A pair of live peregrine falcons roost on a ledge, courtesy of McGill University. Look away, pigeon lovers.

Across Dorchester Boulevard witness a scaled-down version of St. Peter's in the Vatican: **St. James RC** (Maree Rain Doo Moaned). Perched along the ledge are statues of men in long gowns. These are the patron saints of Montreal's parishes. Folklore has it that their faces resemble city councillors of the time. They don't.

Continue along Dorchester between Place Ville-Marie and the **Queen Elizabeth Hotel**. We are now passing through the last of the great downtown "anglocore" completed in the early sixties: **Place Bonaventure, Place Victoria, the C-I-L House**. All of these tell tales of power and the pursuit of wealth. Our story.

We are now at **Beaver Hall Hill**. On your right, **St. Patrick's Cathedral**, built the same year the Irish were dropping off like flies from the plague.

Close by is the stately **Engineer's Club**. Go on in. You're allowed to now because it's a restaurant. Do not try this with the **St. James Club**.

We have now reached the eastern boundary of the tour. The point of no return. Feel apprehensive. Reach for flask.

Up the street is **Phillips Square**, where you will see three reassuring sights:

— the concrete mass of the **Canada Cement Building**. Built in 1922 with foresight and the city's first under-ground garage;
— **Henry Morgan & Co**. A family business, sold to the Hudson Bay Company, now La Baie;
— **La Birk**. For centuries, **Henry Birks & Sons** sup-plied silver tea services and shiny objects in blue boxes to the citizenry of upper Montreal. Check the time on the Roman numeraled clock outside. Go inside and ask to see the bridal registry. Find out Mila Mulroney's pattern. Watch out for the revolving door door door.

Leave Birks and cross the street where you'll find another neogothic anglican. Say hello. Pass **Christ Church Cathedral**. At University, you can see **Eaton**, formerly Eaton's. Further on is **Simpsons**, formerly Simpson's. Legend has it that somewhere in the city there is a warehouse filled with apostrophe esses wait-ing to take their rightful place once again.

Go up **University Street**, straight up the stairs of **Royal Victoria College** into the solid arms of **Queen Victoria**. This marks the beginning of **McGill University**. Enter through the

McRoddick Gates and visit the campus: The McConnell Engineering Building, the McLennan Library, the McBronfman Management Building, and you're out on McTavish Street.

Savour the street names in this stretch: **Stanley, Drummond, Mountain**. Walk briskly down Mountain Street. Ignore the block filled with forgettable French bars. Instead, feast your eyes on the granite mass of **Jas. A. Ogilvy's Ltd.** Since 1879. Ogilvy's is more than a department store, it's a symbol.

Arrive at Ogilvy's in time for "elevensies". In the middle of the store, stop to get your bearings under the over-size chandelier, a relic from **Her Majesty's Theatre**. Breathe in the decidedly Scottish air. Ogilvy's has an impressive display of solid stuff from the British Isles, remnants from royal households and artifacts from various military campaigns. Most of them still alive and working right here.

Ride the elevator with a bekilted female wearing white gloves. She'll tell you where to get off. Head for the **Tartan Room**. Enjoy your tea in comforting surroundings: Starched white linen, sturdy flatware, and those nice touches like a pot of hot water, ribbon sandwiches and white cake.

The tour is now officially at an end.

You have a choice. You can stay and stock up on Kenneth McKeller records and linger until store-closing. You'll be piped out by the staff piper, the skirl of the wondrous instrument for a moment transporting you to the highlands before you hit St. Catherine Street. At rush hour this could prove dangerous. Or: You can leave Ogilvy's now, while it's still light, and retreat to Windsor Station.

The train is waiting for points west: Lachine, Pointe Claire, Beaconsfield, . . . Victoria.

Signing Off

Formerly "Tavern — Taverne"

Formerly "Cookie's Main Lunch"

Formerly "The Magic City Pool Room"

Formerly "Dusty's Restaurant"

Formerly "Schwartz's Montreal Hebrew Delicatessen"

REJECTS FROM *LA RÉGIE*

coupe de grâce. . . . . lawn mower
pas de deux . . . . father of twins
homme d'affaires. . . . . .a gigolo
maison de santé. . . . . Father Christmas's workshop
par exemple. . . . . the perfect father
en famille . . . . .pregnant
garder la foi. . . . . take care of your liver

car pool. . . . . piscine à voiture
hit the road. . . . . frappez la rue
top banana . . . . haute banane
bridge game. . . . . .jeu de pont
Beaver Hall Hill . . . . Montée Castor Corridor

Treason
in The Townships

A Tale of Two Toponymies

Charles Bury

Seems someone up there in Quebec City got the idea to run the municipality of Compton Township through the toponymy machine.

So what happened was one day the Compton town secretary got a letter from La Commission with a suggested list of new names for the dirt and gravel roads of the rambling town. Letter said that as soon as the council passed a resolution changing the names according to the list, La Commission could "officialize the ways of communications", as they put it, of little Com Township.

Weird thing was, all the roads already had names, and had had for as much as a hundred years or more. Of course, all the names were English names — Chemin Ives' Hill, Chemin Huff, Chemin Smith, Chemin Hyatt. Well, the good people of Compton started to wonder what was going on. So they decided a few of them better go to the next council meeting, set for a week from Monday.

The biggest village in Compton Township is Moe's River. And the folks of Moe's River — population a hundred or so on a good day — sent a delegation of about twenty to the meeting. Now, you've got to understand here that although the people of Moe's River are English-speaking, about nine-tenths of Compton Township is French. Council welcomed the delegation, biggest attendance at council in anyone's memory. The mayor said something along the lines that council had been wondering what to do about the letter and was glad to hear what the citizens thought before doing anything about it — a refreshing change in any jurisdiction.

The citizens were only too glad to fill the council in. With a civility little known in larger circles, the representative of the Moe's River Improvement Association (Association pour l'amélioration de Moe's River, *not* association pour l'amélioration de . . . ah, you know what I mean) thanked the mayor and the councillors for the chance to address them and got right down to the point. It seems that in the fine print of the letter, La Commission wasn't being exactly straight. La Commission said, for example, that Chemin Hyatt should be changed to Chemin de la Rivière, because the word Hyatt had "no pertinence to local history". But the people of Moe's River begged to differ. The original Mr. Hyatt, they pointed out, as everyone but La Commission must know, was the man who founded Sherbrooke back in 1811. Once a fabled stop on the mainline of Canadian industry, that city was first called Hyatt's Mills (no, not Moulins Hyatt, as La Commission might dream). But, as almost everybody knows, before Mr. Hyatt went to Sherbrooke, he had lived in Moe's River; more precisely on what later came to be known as Hyatt Road, still later called Chemin Hyatt.

And further down in the small print, La Commission said that the name "Sideleau" would be okay for naming roads because the name "was found in the telephone book"! But what La Commission didn't seem to notice is that there are also some Hyatts in the phone book — not on the same page, maybe, but in the same phone book, and they live here, too.

Council hesitated only long enough for the secretary to read a letter from one local celeb and a telegram from another.

Prof. Edgar Caron, a retired historian from Montreal, living in Moe's River, said the whole idea of changing the names was something horrible, like the Rape of the Sabine Virgins, and what would we, the francophones, say, if in the rest of Canada they proposed to get rid of place names like Lacombe in Alberta, Saint Boniface and Portage La Prairie in Manitoba, and Sault Saint Marie, etc., in Ontario.

Now Bernie St-Laurent is one of those guys, you don't really know if he's French or English, you know? Sort of like the Eastern Townships region itself, and like his great-uncle who became prime minister of Canada, and who also came from Compton. Bernie is from Moe's River but he made it big and is now a famous star — at least in Compton Station — with the CBC radio-news, eh? Bernie sent a telegram to the council reminding them of all the small-town things they stood for — like representing the citizens. Everyone, even the town secretary, clapped.

Everyone had spoken. Now it was time to act. With the weight of numbers and the force of righteous indignation, council, in a unanimous decision, thanked La Commission very much for their letter and their interest in the tiny municipality. But, said council, we reject your suggestions in their entirety. As if to rub it in, council went a step further and decided to change the name of Chemin Gabriel Lapointe to Chemin Duffy.

The lesson in this story is this: You can send all the letters you want, but you can't take the Hyatt out of Compton.

TRUTH IS STRANGER THAN FICTION . . .

CARRÉ AU CHOCOLAT, n.m. Petit gâteau de forme rectangulaire, aromatisé au chocolat, dont la texture se situe entre le biscuit sec et le gâteau spongieux.
ANGLAIS: BROWNIE

Exerpted from *Répertoire des avis linguistiques et terminologiques* published by *Office de la langue française.*

Test Your A.Q.
(Anglo Quotient)

Are You *Licensed to Speak English?*

Graeme Decarie

In the near future, an unpublished section of Bill 101 will come into effect, requiring those Quebecers who wish to register as anglophones to write an examination. The purpose of this exam will be to ensure that they have an adequate AQ (Anglo Quotient). Officially, scores will be graded as follows:

Perfect score — registered anglophone
One error — conditional anglophone; may speak English only in prayer.
Two or more errors — bienvenue au Québec français.

The following AQ questions have been leaked from government files. Test your AQ now.

1. When General Wolfe was killed, a Scotsman, General Murray, negotiated the surrender of Quebec for the British. Give the national ancestry and name of the man who negotiated for the French.

2.   A young anglophone Quebecer of the 19th century might have put on a blue hat to engage in his favourite sport. What was that sport?

3.   There is a street in Montreal which is named after the father of a Hollywood star of the 1920s, 30s and 40s. Name the street and the star.

4.   What was the first non-Catholic place of worship in Montreal?

5.   A major league baseball player, born in Ontario, retired to open a tavern in Montreal after a career in which he posted the highest batting average ever recorded. What was his name? Hint: A prominent American politician was named after him.

6.   What beverage, invented for which Quebec sporting festival, went on to become a big hit in Britain?

7.   If you had ever met Sir William Macdonald, founder of Macdonald Tobacco, what brand of cigarette should you have offered him?

8.   What Prime Minister of Canada, an anglophone Quebecer, once signed a petition advocating that Canada join the United States?

9.   After Smith, what is the most common name of anglo origin in Quebec?

10.   In the so-called Papineau Rebellion of 1837, rebel forces defeated British troops at the village of St. Denis. Name the rebel commander in that battle.

11.   What Montreal family gave its name to a medical centre and a sports trophy?

12. If you had been an anglo-Quebecer living in 1867, you would probably have been:
a) an urban businessman   b) an urban worker   c) a farmer

13. In 1849, the parliament of Canada was situated in Montreal. It was burned to the ground by a mob of angry anglos. One of the leaders of that mob was Alfred Perry. What was his occupation?

14. Alvina Fuhrer was well known to prominent Montrealers in the latter part of the 19th century for her professional services. What was her profession?

15. Why is Blue Bonnets racetrack called Blue Bonnets?

16. The Cathedral of Notre Dame has for many years been a symbol of the importance of Roman Catholicism in a French Quebec. Who designed it?

17. What man (an anglo) has the most communities in Quebec named after him?

18. Philips Square in Montreal was named, not surprisingly, after a Mr. Phillips. What was his accomplishment that caused the city to name a square after him?

19. What national origin was most common among anglophone Quebecers at the time of Confederation?

20. What national origin is most common among anglophone Quebecers today?

21. What well known Protestant church in Montreal has a tower that appears to be of stone but is really made of aluminum?

22. Montreal's leading Presbyterian newspaper of the 19th century was called *The Witness.* When Irish Catholics started a competing newspaper, what did they call it?

23. What was the name of the first published novel written in the English language in Quebec? (Would it help to know that it was the first published novel written in any language in all of North America?)

24. We all know that the church of Mary, Queen of the World (on Dorchester St.) is a scale model of St. Peter's in Rome. But why is it a scale model of St. Peter's?

25. In 1876, George Stephen, of Bank of Montreal and C.P.R. fame (his home is now the Mount Stephen Club on Drummond St.), turned down a young inventor who was looking for financial backers. What was the young inventor's name?

26. The first National Hockey League player to wear glasses was an anglo-Quebecer. Who was he?

27. Duels were common in New France, and continued after the British conquest until well into the 19th century. But there was a difference between the British and the French styles of duelling. What was it?

28. Blacks have come to Quebec since the earliest days of European settlement as, among other roles, interpreters, slaves, and United Empire Loyalists. Who was the first black to come to Quebec to work as a professional athlete?

29. In 1782, a British naval captain abandoned his ship in the St. Lawrence river to visit his sixteen-year-old sweetheart at Quebec. Only the intervention of friends saved him from court martial and disgrace. Who was he?

30. In 1834, an organization of francophones and anglophones was inaugurated at Montreal with toasts drunk to the King. What was the name of the organization?

ANSWERS

1.   Another Scotsman. Jean-Baptiste-Nicholas-Roch, negotiated for the French. He was descended from the de Ramezay family, originally Ramsay, which migrated from Scotland to France in the 16th century. Thus, two Scotsmen negotiated the surrender of Quebec.

2.   The blue tuque was a badge of membership in the Montreal Snowshoe Club.

3.   Norma Shearer's father owned a factory on what is now Shearer Street.

4.   The Spanish and Portuguese Synagogue.

5.   Tip O'Neill. In fairness, you should know that his batting average belongs to the days before the modern game.

6.   **Bovril** was invented for the Montreal Winter Carnival in the 1880s. A failure here, it did better in Britain.

7.   Just a handshake would have been fine. Sir William disapproved of smoking.

8.   Sir John Abbott, a native of St. Andrew's East, was Prime Minister from 1891 to 1892. He signed the petition in 1849.

9.   Langlois. The name is believed to be a corruption of l'anglais, "the English one".

10.   Wolfred Nelson. Contrary to popular belief, there were many anglophones on the rebel side, just as there were many francophones on the government side.

11.   The Allan family gave its name to the Allan Memorial, originally the family home, and to the Allan Cup for amateur hockey.

12. Despite a widespread notion that anglo-Quebecers are and always have been businessmen, in 1867, the overwhelming majority were farmers. Those in the urban working class were a distant second — and the urban businessmen a remote third.

13. He was Montreal's Fire Chief.

14. According to her autobiography, she was a midwife who specialized in attending to the unwed daughters of the wealthy.

15. This racetrack was originally in Montreal West, near the spot where Scottish soldiers were stationed during the War of 1812. The soldiers wore blue bonnets.

16. James O'Donnell, an American Protestant of Irish descent.

17. Charles Lennox, Duke of Richmond, who was the Governor from 1818 to 1819, inspired the names of three communities in Quebec — Richmond, New Richmond, and Lennoxville. A fourth, Richmond Hill, is in Ontario.

18. Nothing in particular. Mr. Phillips was a businessman and city councillor whose heirs transferred the land to the city in 1842.

19. Irish.

20. Canadian, of course. However, if you consider ancestry, the Italians are in the lead. The English have never been the largest group.

21. Christ Church Cathedral. The original stone tower was replaced when it threatened to topple of its own weight.

22. *The True Witness.*

23. *The History of Emily Montague* was written at Quebec by Frances Brooke, the wife of a British army chaplain. It was published in England in 1769.

24. Bishop Ignace Bourget intended it as a reminder that the Pope ruled supreme, even in Montreal. Dorchester Street was then the centre of an English Protestant residential district.

25. Alexander Graham Bell.

26. Russ Blinco.

27. The French duelled with swords, the English with pistols. There is no record of bicultural duelling.

28. Herb Trawick, who came to star with the Montreal Alouettes.

29. Horatio Nelson.

30. The Saint Jean Baptiste Society.

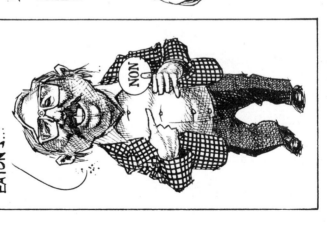

"BICULTURAL"

Tired of being told that you're living in the most exciting city in North America when you know that the wildest thing you've done in the last three years was to be late for the kids' Christmas pageant?

Do you feel that somehow there's more to Montreal nightlife than the Beaconsfield bake sale or a rare night at the Beth Tikvah players?

Have you, in fact, been sorely tempted to cash in on all those years of French classes and go for a drink on St. Denis street, . . . but you're afraid that you'll dress all wrong, say the wrong things and end up being insulted, or even worse, ignored? Well, stop worrying and start reading:

Stepping H'Out

Tripping the Light Fantastique

Wayne Grigsby and Katie Malloch

In any other city in the world, stepping out is simple. Just twist the knob, swing wide the door, and sally forth — to a restaurant, a bar, a movie, the theatre, whatever. But for Quebec anglos, life just ain't that simple.

Where you're going and who will be there will make all the difference in what and how you eat, drink, smoke, dress, watch, sing, walk, talk, court or sport. Let's start with the basics.

DRESS

How you dress depends on where you're going. In general, you needn't bother dressing sensibly — getting a lot of wear out of an outfit gets you no Brownie points here. Spend money on clothes (you'll be surprised to find how good it feels). Make-up is extremely important and infinitely complex in Quebec. If in doubt, take lessons. And for God's sake, don't be caught wearing blue eyeshadow. Another rule of thumb concerns fur coats and jewellery — buy the best and wear it proudly. Modesty is boring.

West of Bleury

Dress the way your mother taught you. In case your mother didn't bother, pick up any old fashion magazine from Cleveland or Toronto.

Fringes of Outremont

Chic is de rigueur. Aim for the cover of *Vogue* or *Marie-Claire.* But be alert: The look will change every six months. Use the formal "vous" in this part of town.

North of St. Louis Square

Welcome to the land of left-over bell-bottom jeans, tie-dye headbands, and the complete works of Jimi Hendrix. Punctuate sentences with "t'sé que je veux dire, man?" (tséquejvedzire, man?). Translation: "Like, you know what I mean, man?"

East of Papineau

Trash with flash rules here. Wear terrycloth short-shorts, four-inch heels, puce singlets, and make sure you've got fuzzy dice dangling from your car's rear-view mirror. Garish medallions can still be found dangling on the bellies of men wearing

★★★

turtlenecks and white belts (that match their white shoes). Don't snicker — these men could be Créditiste leadership candidates.

THE THEATRE

Going to the theatre used to be extremely intimidating, especially in the heyday of Michel Tremblay. Even a whisper of English in the lobby could bring on withering looks. But take heart. Things have changed! Nowadays, most French theatre in Quebec is hand-me-down Broadway — translated and adapted, of course, but second-hand nonetheless. So it is now okay to kill time in the lobby or bar line-up by comparing the Jean Duceppe production of *The Sunshine Boys* with the one you saw in New York — you can even do it in English.

A kiss on both cheeks to those anglos who have seen *Broue* in the original (preferably at the cubby hole Théâtre de Voyagements), or who know that *Pied-de-poule* is a smash hit musical which has nothing whatsoever to do with chicken feet.

THE MOVIES

Always arrive late for the movies — everyone else will. Be prepared for talkers, especially in Woody Allen films where *everything* needs translation and discussion.

Say "le cinéma" when speaking of good movies, use "les vues" when you're just going out to catch a flick.

Keep your starlets straight: Geneviève Bujold is completely passée, Carole Laure's star is fading, and Gabrielle Lazure's is rising, despite the fact that her father (Denis) is a PQ cabinet minister.

★★

Be prepared to be serious about movies. Fellini, Truffaut, Herzog, Lelouch and Godard are considered to be infinitely more important than Spielberg and Lucas. (Isn't it nice to live in a culture that doesn't take *People* magazine for gospel?)

THE BARS, BISTROS, CLUBS AND CAFÉS

The trick here is insouciance — be debonair about drinking, lounging, smoking, talking and picking the right clothes. You may find it difficult to get the hang of it right away, but it is well worth the effort.

A note of caution: Crescent Street may be easy, but lines like "Come here often"? will get you laughed off la Rue St. Denis. Cruising on this street is a matter of glances, half-smiles and cadging a Gitane.

Order beer or red wine (anglos give themselves away by ordering white wine or worse, spritzers). Talk about affairs of the heart or third world politics. Look mournful whenever Quebec politics are mentioned.

Should you find yourself in a small café that serves fruit juices and herbal teas — watch out! Serious discussion of U.S. policy in the middle East, Latin America and Asia is just a table away. Call the Parti Québecois reactionary sell-outs and heads will nod sagely. However, unless your clothes are woven in Peru or sold in surplus stores, you will be taken for someone from *Le Devoir* slumming.

Biker bars can, believe it or not, be great places for anglos who can't speak French, since nobody speaks at all. Guys should wear t-shirts, jeans and leather jackets; molls replace the t-shirt with a halter top. Decals can be used to simulate tatoos.

★★

MUSIC

Learn to be eclectic: Be well versed in old rock, art rock, jazz and Québecois traditional. Why? Because Elvis sold more records per capita in Quebec than anywhere else in the world. Because Pink Floyd was popular here long before LA caught on to them. Because jazz has become hugely popular through the International Jazz Festival held here every July. Québecois traditional? Don't let it scare you — it's all based on Scottish and Irish fiddle music. So play 'em your Don Messer records and gloat.

Learn to dance — Quebecers are dancin' fools. Ballroom, jitterbug, jive and step dancing live on here even though the rest of North America has given them up for slam dancing. Dipping is de rigeur and a fluent *paso doble* will charm the birds right out of the trees — even in a disco.

Learn to hum — maybe a little Mozart or an aria or two from one of the major Italian operas. This is not square, this is sophisticated and will do more for the end of an evening than a boatload of Johnny Mathis.

Remember:
— Robert Charlebois is over the hill
— only grannies like René or Nathalie Simard
— chansonniers, with the exception of Felix Leclerc and Gilles Vigneault, are totally passé, we mean *totally*
— the less said about Pierre Lalonde, the better.

EATING OUT

This is the most paradoxical question you will have to face in the new Quebec. While stuffing their faces with frites, hot dogs steamés and a gros Mac, Montrealers will maintain that they have the finest restaurants and the finest palates in North America. Instinctively, they understand the subtle complexities of haute cuisine, yet they settle for the most mediocre Italian and Chinese food. We haven't been able to solve these riddles, but we have observed what seem to be some general principles:

— eat late
— ignore the menu; make the waiter run it through for you
— gravy on french fries is okay at lunch, tacky at dinner
— break all the rules: Have red wine with fish, mop up the sauce with a chunk of bread, dunk your croissant in your café-au-lait, buy the chef a drink, talk with your mouth full. In short, don't hold back — enjoy!
— don't worry about the noise level. Only les anglais treat dining out as if it were some sort of memorial service.

Taverns and brasseries are great places for a night away from it all. *Never* talk about anything more controversial than the Expos, the Canadiens, or the high cost of beer. Order a "gros mol' ". A quart stays colder longer than "deux draff' ". Only panty-waist civil servants order light beers. Know ten names from the '55 - '60 Canadiens' roster. Eat the pig knuckles. Walk into the wind on the way home.

Le Jacques Strap

How to Become
a French Athletic Supporter

Michael Farber and Mike Boone

LE BASEBALL

There is a warning, stencilled in black letters on the wall
behind home plate in the Olympic Stadium, that violates every
principle of Quebec society. The admonition reads: "No pepper". It may be the last unilingual English sign in Quebec; and it
is on display in a facility owned and administered by the
provincial government.

The dilemma which confronts the stadium's managers is
that "No pepper" does not translate into French. "Pas de
poivre" doesn't mean anything to anyone.

"Pepper" is a pre-game exercise in which baseball players
toss balls at a batter, who gently taps them back. In French, this
is called "le pepper game" — a franglais phrase which typifies
the uneasy marriage between the French language and an American sport adored by millions of francophones.

Here are a few hopelessly awkward words and phrases used by French TV announcers and visitors from Lyons watching their first baseball game:

La chandelle — A lazy fly ball. Literally translated, "the candle", which makes no sense whatever. In English, a lazy fly ball is known as "a can of corn".

Frappeur d'urgence — Pinch-hitter. The French phrase does add a certain drama and immediacy to the act of pinch-hitting. You half-expect to see the "frappeur d'urgence" come to the plate in an ambulance.

Grand chelem — Grand slam. The phrase, used to describe a bases-loaded home run, is derived from the grand slam in bridge, a game francophones played before Montreal got the Expos.

Grand chelem is not to be confused with "Grand shalom", which describes the exodus from Olympic Stadium box seats in the late innings of afternoon games preceding Yom Kippur.

Le gérant — Manager. When Jim Fanning, the affable but inexperienced Expos executive, managed the team for the final month of the 1981 season, he was known as the Jolly Green Gérant.

Le hot dog — apparently this is French for a "steamie".

Mauvais lancer — Wild pitch. The literal translation, bad pitch, is inexact. A bad pitch misses the strike zone by three inches; a wild pitch misses the catcher by eight feet.

Retrait sur des prises — A strikeout. (A spendid example of using four words where one has sufficed since Ty Cobb was in diapers.) When a third strike is called and the batter is shocked by the umpire's decision, it is known as a "retrait surprise".

Le Grand Orange — nickname of Rusty Staub, a popular outfielder who played for the Expos in the formative years of the franchise.

Le Gros Orange — Youppi!

Le Stade — The Olympic Stadium. Many English sportswriters refer to this grotesque hunk of architectural folly as the Big O, the Big Owe or Taillebert's Mistake. It is the tragic result of Montreal Mayor Jean Drapeau's "Édifice Complex". Most French writers, however, play it straight and call the stadium "le stade". No sense of gallows humour among that lot.

La foule — The crowd. Considering the cost of tickets, parking, refreshments and souvenirs at a baseball game in Montreal, la foule and its money are soon parted.

Shoo! — Boo! French fans do not boo during bad plays, they shoo. As in "Shoo! Shoo! . . . ya dumb jerk!" Maybe the fans can tell the difference, but it sounds the same to the players.

LE HOCKEY

The Montreal Canadiens, with 21 Stanley Cup wins, are the most successful team in the history of the National Hockey League. Season's tickets belonging to deceased Canadiens' fans are the subject of ugly probate battles among inheritors.

Until the Quebec Nordiques entered the NHL with an almost one hundred percent francophone roster and uniforms festooned with fleur-de-lys, the Montreal Canadiens were THE hockey team of the province.

Dubbed the Flying Frenchmen, le Club de Hockey Canadien sometimes is known as Les Tricolores, in recognition of its red, blue and white uniforms, or Les Glorieux. The Office de la langue française, however, is expected to recommend whether or not the Canadiens can still be referred to as Les Glorieux after being eliminated in the first round of the Stanley Cup playoffs for the last three years.

The coach of the Canadiens is Bob Berry, who grew up in the Town of Mount Royal. When he was initially hired by the Canadiens, some French talk-show callers suggested he change his name to Bob Berri.

Here are a few French terms for fans at the Forum:

Bataille, Escarmouche, Bagarre générale — The three stages of mindless hockey violence. A *bataille* is generally waged by two players with no outside interference. When a third party joins the fracas, it escalates into an *escarmouche*. This is often the signal for every player on the ice to drop his gloves and go at it; the ensuing obscene spectacle is your basic Pier Six *bagarre générale.*

Dans les filets — this means "in the nets" and has nothing to do with the fish sandwiches on sesame seed buns being served at the fast-food emporium across the street from the Forum.

La Glace — the ice, the playing surface. When leading Canadiens enforcer Chris Nilan takes on a tough from the opposition and all hell breaks loose, this is known as a "glace menagerie".

Lance et conte — the equivalent of "he shoots, he scores!". Actually, Molson Breweries, owner of the Canadiens, is upset because this popular French phrase sounds too much like "lance ciquante" — "shoot 50", 50 being the name of a beer brewed by rival Labatt. Next season the company may direct all French announcers to say "lance et Mol' " whenever a goal is scored.

La rondelle — the puck. An American friend, watching *La Soirée du Hockey* for the first time, said he realized there were a lot of French people in Montreal but still couldn't understand why every hockey player was named La Rondelle.

Le Joual

The True Story...
Finally Told in English

Gerry Bergeron

You know that awful feeling that comes from losing your way in deepest "East-end". "Oh, Christ! I'm going to have to ask for directions." First you get a cup of coffee to sharpen your concentration. Then, taking a deep breath, you say "Eskewzay-mwa, m'syer, oo ay le metro?"

Like lead from a shotgun, the answer zings past your unattuned anglo ears: "B'en poigne 'citte tou drette ch'qu'à'a trac, vir à drette, p'i c'est drette là." "Right, so much for that", you think to yourself, wandering off hopelessly.

Joual. To those who speak it, it's a language. To a Parisien it is a quaint dialect. To the Outremont francophone, it is a colourful "langage populaire" that inspires the same pride for cultural heritage that Eskimo sculpture inspires in fashionable Torontonians.

To the anglophone, it might as well be a secret code.

All francophone Quebecers understand *joual*, even if they don't actually practice it. Anglophones don't understand it at all. In fact, they can't. *Joual* is a genetic trait and anglos are missing the vital chromosome. If that doesn't relieve your feelings of inadequacy, take heart: in France, Québecois films are often sub-titled.

Here is a glossary of terms and expressions that may help the next time you get stranded "out there";

LEVEL A: BEGINNER'S JOUAL FOR THE ANGLOPHONE

JOUAL	ENGLISH
le driveshaff	the driveshaft
le crankshaff	the crankshaft
la crankcase	the crankcase
le muffleur	the muffler
l'ighway	the highway
le foreman	the foreman
les choques	the shock absorbers
le toune-oppe	the tune-up
puncher	to report for work
le tailleur	the tire
la beaute	the bolt
tailleter	to tighten
tailleter les beautes	to tighten the bolts
le rentche	the wrench
le rentche à ratshit	the ratchet wrench
le creaubaure	the crowbar
la slutch	the slush
un botche	the cigarette butt
le char	the car (informal)
la machine	the car (formal)

LEVEL B: INTERMEDIATE JOUAL

JOUAL	ENGLISH
dewowr	outside
frette	cold
'haud	hot
chose là	whatchamacallit
slaqué	laid off (from work)
s'a sly	on the sly (moonlighting)
drette	straight
à drette	right (as in turn right)
'citte	here
a'c	with
i'	he
a	she
ayaille (a-yoi)	ouch
poigné (pun-yay)	angst
chu poigné	I am filled with angst
c'pas catholique	it's not kosher
le joual	the horse
les canayens	*French*-canadians (archaic; pre-1960)
les anglais	anyone else
au quai	okay
eniwé	nevertheless, anyway
dat's owl	c'est tout

LEVEL C: INACCESSIBLE JOUAL

JOUAL (FRENCH)	ENGLISH
fa frette dewowr (il fait froid dehors)	**it's** cold outside
fa 'haud 'citte (il fait chaud ici)	it's hot here
i'm cré p'us (il ne me croit plus)	he doesn't believe me anymore
a'l' cré p'us (elle ne le croit plus)	she doesn't believe him anymore
m'omme débroiller (je vais me débroiller)	I'll get by
m'eq' i' arrive, tsu p'êt sure qui'i v'en manger une bonne (Mais quand il arrive tu peut être sur qu'il va en manger une bonne)	when he arrives you may be sure that he'll get what's coming to him
ayou qu'c'est 'arue Pine? (Où est-ce que c'est l'avenue des Pins?)	where is Pine Avenue?
c'pas ma job	it's out of my jurisdiction
b'en poigne 'citte tou drette ch' qu'à'a trac, vir à drette, p'i c'est drette là (see page 1)	well, continue along this street until the railroad tracks, turn right, and there your are

---

Two anglos were visiting Montreal from Toronto. They desperately wanted to "fit in", so they asked a friend to teach them how to order in a restaurant, "just like a Québecois". The friend complied.

The next day, the two anglos were walking down St. Hubert St. and stormed into an establishment to order lunch and to try out their lesson.

"Donne-moy quat' 'otdog, halldress, pis trois frites et quat' pepsi, tabernacle!" thundered one of the anglos, beating his fist on the counter. "Pis un Maywest!"

But the man behind the counter just shrugged.

"Etes-vous anglais?" he inquired. "Are you English?"

"Uh, . . . yeah," said the crestfallen anglo. "How could you tell?"

"Well," said the man behind the counter. "This is a hardware store."

Le Mot Final

From One Minority to Another

Serge Grenier

TUESDAY

You are worried because you are a minority. Well, it is true
. . . you are a minority. But I am a minority, too. So are Pierre
Trudeau and René Levesque. Camille Laurin, thank God! is
a minority. We all are. Can you imagine the traffic jam on
the 401 when all minorities decide to move to Toronto? Some
of them, I'm afraid, might have to settle down in Sudbury or
North Bay. La solution? L'unique solution? Demeurer à Montréal ou, si vous insistez absolument, à Dollard-des-Ormeaux.

Voici un bref aperçu des villes canadiennes où vous seriez
malheureux comme les pierres (as unhappy as stones). If you've
already left Montreal, you probably are. D'abord, Saint-Jean de
Terreneuve, as we call it, is best avoided unless you want to sail
your boat on Lake Quidi Vidi for the rest of your life. Halifax:
A major disaster hit Halifax in 1917. You could be the next
one. New Brunswick: There are no cities in New Brunswick.
Winnipeg: La ville de Winnipeg est le centre géographique du
Canada. And frankly, who cares? Seriez-vous intéressé par la
Saskatchewan? Think twice: There's no Perrier in Moose Jaw.
Calgary, Edmonton, Vancouver: Why not Australia? Toronto:
Oh, Toronto! Croyez-vous vraiment que Toronto est la métro-
pole du Canada? Some of your best friends moved to Toronto.
Look at them: Levé tôt, couché tôt, forty-five minutes for

lunch, work, work, work. C'est une vie, ça? C'est une métro-pole, ça? If you're still mourning for your great-aunt who was buried with her adornments of the Imperial Order of the Daughters of the Empire, Toronto est à vous.

Ottawa représente un cas particulier. I'm sure you wouldn't like it; it's damp. According to the *National Geographic Maga-zine* (January, 1979), Ottawa and Oulan Bator (Mongolia) are the two coldest capital cities in the world. It's very damp. Imaginez un week-end à Ottawa: A boat ride on the Rideau canal, a visit to the National Museum of Anthropology, your photo being taken by Yousuf Karsh. Now, imagine the other weekends.

Partir, oui, mais pour aller où? Avouez plutôt que vous adorez Montréal et que vous seriez incapable de vous en passer. Avouez! Admit that you are moved by 40,000 Montréalais, au stade Olympique pour un match des Expos, se tiennent debout et chantent ensemble, les Francos en français, les Anglos en anglais, le O Canada, une bière dans une main, un hot dog dans l'autre.

MERCREDI

You are a fossil if you still refer to Québec as Lower Can-ada. If more than two of your relatives still play the bagpipes. If you think Frank Hanley should run again as an MNA. If, to you, Jacques-Cartier is a bridge and nothing but a bridge. If you still call Boulevard de Maisonneuve Burnside Street. If you pre-tend to ignore that Laval-sur-le-Lac is part of Ville de Laval. If you believe that Marguerite Corriveau was born in Liverpool.

I am a fossil if I have said once or twice, even a long time ago, "les maudits Anglais". If I am a member of Société Saint-Jean-Baptiste. If I think you eat boiled beef, drink flat beer and dress with the finesse of a snow tire. If I think that Alliance Québec is a matrimonial agency.

THURSDAY

You are a Montrealer, you have a good job, you live at La Cité, you think you speak some French, you would love to pick up a French girl on Saint-Denis or Prince Arthur. You spot one. Unfortunately, your spoken French is not as good as it used to be, but you still order deux bières. If you look like Tom Selleck, you'll make love like animals and no translation will be needed for *aaaaggghhhh*. If you're the Ed McMahon type, don't waste time trying to build a decent sentence with words such as "cherchez la femme", "déja vu", "détente" or "maitre d' ". If you hang around Stanley Street, simply remember that herpès is herpes and SIDA is AIDS. One golden rule: s'il vous plaît, pas de Parisian French. Je vous promets de ne pas vous parler de London English.

VENDREDI

You are a Montréalais. Vous avez un loft rue Saint-Paul ou un appartement rue Esplanade. Vous avez de l'admiration pour Jean Drapeau but you're a member of MAG or MCM. Il y a des bons films au Seville. Your thought of the day is: Real Montrealers do eat quiche on Crescent Street. John Warden et Michel Robichaud, très jolis, mais vous préférez le Place Ville Marie Look (Milton Park Chic?). Vous achetez votre Sunday edition of *The New York Times* chez International News rue Peel. You do your thing the Village Lincoln way. Vous buvez du café Van Houtte. You wrote a song: I wag my chin at Peel and St. Catherine / I don't blow my horn at Bloor and Yonge. Ah, un week-end dans les Townships ou du ski à Mont-Tremblant!

SAMEDI

Levi's, t-shirt, Adidas ou vos Kodiak de La Ouèrâsse. Le shopping. Un mohair chez Ogilvy. Ham (Buywell? L'Epicurien?) for tomorrow's Eggs Benedict. And guess who's *not* coming to dinner: Eric Maldoff — so Art Deco; Mordecai Richler —

Saint Urbain Colonial; Joan Dougherty — Early Victorian. Everybody from *Snow Job*: Any furniture from Pascal. And that twit from CBM-FM who mispronounced Charles Dutoit. Please add Léandre Bergeron, François-Albert Angers and Patsy Gallant.

Chances are we'll meet at Waldman's — we both love rouget (red snapper) and crevettes de Matane (crevettes de Matane), don't we? Or we could have a few beers in a tavern, among men. Your French is excellent with only minor problems using "tu" and "vous". And remember: A ship is masculine, a car is feminine and Douglas Leopold is bilingual. We'll agree on Robert Bourassa (nous n'avons pas le choix), defeat Pierre Trudeau and replace him with another Montréalais, and demonstrate that we are the only truly Canadian Canadians in Canada.

Well, mon ami, I must tell you this: I lived in Ottawa and Toronto for five years. Heureux d'être de retour. Happy to be back. C'était agréable de manger chez Fenton's de temps en temps, but I'd rather have dinner with you aux Halles, chez Abacus, au Pavillon de l'Atlantique, á la Troika, à La Sila, au Katsura, ou chez Schwartz. Nous pourrons alors discuter de l'avenir du pays, de l'élection d'un Anglo (Phyllis Lambert?) à la mairie de Montréal. And we'll joke. Is Jean Chrétien biodegradable? Do Albertans have a soul?

The Anglo Integration Quiz

Well, you've had 143 pages to get the hang of living in Quebec (139 pages if you didn't read "Le Mot Final").

Now, let's see if you've learned anything.

1. A réveillon is:

a) A Christmas Eve festivity
b) The alarm setting on your digital watch
c) A motel on Sherbrooke St. East

2. 21:00 refers to:

a) A disco on St. Denis Street
b) The departure time for the train to Toronto
c) 9 o'clock p.m.

3. What is an "omble chevalier"?

a) A horsefly
b) A horsemeat omelette
c) An arctic char

4. What is the most important event in Québec Anglo history?

a) The Battle on the Plains of Abraham
b) The day Murrays restaurant served its first steamed fruit pudding
c) The Yvette rally
d) The great anglo uprising after the proposed cancellation of the trains to the West Island
e) All of the above

5. Léo Chevalier is:

a) A hockey player
b) A fashion designer
c) Maurice Chevalier's real name

6. "Fêves" are to "Lard" as:

a) Tea is to crumpets
b) "Maudit" is to "Anglais"
c) Pork is to beans

7. "Croutons" go:

a) On your salad
b) On your shoes
c) Around the windshield of your car

8. Give yourself 5 points if you know whether you wear a "redingote" or a "boulingrin".

9. "Le petit hareng" is:

a) A brief lecture
b) A short cocktail dress
c) A herring

10. A "hambourgeois" is:

a) More expensive than a hamburger
b) Less expensive than a sirloin steak
c) A member of the new Québecois middle class

11. "J'ai mon voyage" means:

a) I've got my tickets for Florida
b) Now I've seen everything
c) What a trip, man

12. CLSC stands for:

a) A French-language radio station
b) A community health clinic
c) Camille Laurin Salon de Coiffeur

13. Jonquière is:

a) A metro stop in Montréal Est
b) A shampoo
c) Chicoutimi's twin city

14. A "naturopath" is:

a) A hiking trail
b) An organic killer
c) Someone who deals in herbal remedies

15. "Je me souviens" refers to:

a) The glory of the French regime
b) The Dubois brothers' motto
c) A perfume
d) I forget

16. Name the most famous Bill in Quebec:

a) Bill 101
b) Bill 111
c) Bill Wong

17. A "cabane à sucre" is:

a) A sugar-daddy's condo
b) A health spa
c) A place where maple syrup is made

18. Gabrielle Roy was:

a) A famous visagiste
b) The PQ MNA for Repentigny
c) An award-winning author

19. Pie IX is:

a) One more pie-in-the-sky loto
b) A new recipe from Mme Benoit
c) A metro stop for the Big "O"

20. Give yourself 9 points if you always knew how to pronounce Pie IX.

21. What is Québec's best-known export?

a) Maple syrup
b) Pine furniture
c) Anglophones

22. Why should Anglos stay in Québec?

a) The OLF employees need their jobs
b) Someone's got to maintain the tradition of making real tea
c) Because it's home

23. Give yourself 5 points if you know whether or not St. Louis de Ha-Ha really exists.

ANSWERS

1. (a) A réveillon is a festive meal held after midnight mass on Christmas Eve.   5

2. (c) This is the international time system.   6

3. (c) An "omble chevalier" is the new, improved translation for arctic char. The OLF will be pleased with you.   7

4. (e) All of the above. Why be choosy?   10

5. (b) Léo Chevalier is a designer from Quebec. Congratulations, you're more aware of fashion than most anglos.   5

6. (c) If you chose (b), deduct 6 points for being too paranoid.   5

7. (a) "Croutons" go on your salad. If you thought (c) was correct, you're trying too hard.   5

8. You wear a "redingote." Deduct all 5 points if you pronounced it "ridingcoat." A "boulingrin" is a bowling green.   5

9. (c) A herring. The OLF will be pleased, but no one else will care if you know this.   2

10. (a) A "hambourgeois" is more expensive than a hamburger. Someone has to pay for the printing costs of the new menus.   5

11. (b) This is an expression you'll be able to use often in Quebec.   2

12. (b) The CLSC are community health clinics. Give yourself an extra 5 points for having basic survival skills.   10

13. (c) Chicoutimi's twin city. Also known in some circles as the "Paris of the North".   2

14. (c) Give yourself 1 point if you're visiting from B.C. and you guessed (b).   5

15. (a) This line first appeared in 1883 in a work by Eugène Taché. Deduct 5 points if you thought it only appeared on your licence plate.   5

16. (c) The Bill with the most TV coverage.   5

17. (c) Any tourist knows this.   1

18. (c) You can fake it and read her books in English translation.   5

19. (c) Also the name of the boulevard to the west of the Big O.   4

20. Pee-neuf.   9

21. (a) Don't ask which is second.   5

22. (c) of course. Deduct 5 point if you said it wistfully.   15

23. St. Louis de Ha-Ha really does exist.

WHAT YOUR SCORE MEANS

100–130 — Merveilleux! Formidable! C'est too much!

50–99 — Very good! There's a quiche in the mail for you.

25–49 — Pas mal, but not good. No *cigare* for you.

24 or less — Go back to page one and start over. This time read *all* of *Le Mot Final.*

What's the best thing anglophones have to offer Quebec?
"Vertical and venetian blinds."
Stephen and David Shiller, owners of *Au Bon Marché*

Who's your favourite anglophone cultural hero?
"The Great Antonio whose feat of pulling five buses at a time transcends all linguistic and cultural barriers."
Tommy Schnurmacher, columnist for *The Gazette*

How can you tell the difference between an anglophone and a franco-phone?
"The anglo is the one carrying *Le Devoir.*"
Don McGowan, Host of CTV's *McGowan's World*

What do you like best about Montreal?
"Lafleur's hot dogs and Jean Drapeau."
Why Jean Drapeau?
"He helps me spend my money."
Aaron Rand, CKGM Radio